SpringerBriefs in Education

We are delighted to announce SpringerBriefs in Education, an innovative product type that combines elements of both journals and books. Briefs present concise summaries of cutting-edge research and practical applications in education. Featuring compact volumes of 50 to 125 pages, the SpringerBriefs in Education allow authors to present their ideas and readers to absorb them with a minimal time investment. Briefs are published as part of Springer's eBook Collection. In addition, Briefs are available for individual print and electronic purchase.

SpringerBriefs in Education cover a broad range of educational fields such as: Science Education, Higher Education, Educational Psychology, Assessment & Evaluation, Language Education, Mathematics Education, Educational Technology, Medical Education and Educational Policy.

SpringerBriefs typically offer an outlet for:

- An introduction to a (sub)field in education summarizing and giving an overview of theories, issues, core concepts and/or key literature in a particular field
- A timely report of state-of-the art analytical techniques and instruments in the field of educational research
- A presentation of core educational concepts
- An overview of a testing and evaluation method
- A snapshot of a hot or emerging topic or policy change
- An in-depth case study
- A literature review
- A report/review study of a survey
- An elaborated thesis

Both solicited and unsolicited manuscripts are considered for publication in the SpringerBriefs in Education series. Potential authors are warmly invited to complete and submit the Briefs Author Proposal form. All projects will be submitted to editorial review by editorial advisors.

SpringerBriefs are characterized by expedited production schedules with the aim for publication 8 to 12 weeks after acceptance and fast, global electronic dissemination through our online platform SpringerLink. The standard concise author contracts guarantee that:

- an individual ISBN is assigned to each manuscript
- each manuscript is copyrighted in the name of the author
- the author retains the right to post the pre-publication version on his/her website or that of his/her institution

More information about this series at http://www.springer.com/series/8914

John Willison

The Models of Engaged Learning and Teaching

Connecting Sophisticated Thinking
from Early Childhood to PhD

 Springer Open

John Willison
The University of Adelaide
Adelaide, SA, Australia

ISSN 2211-1921   ISSN 2211-193X (electronic)
SpringerBriefs in Education
ISBN 978-981-15-2682-4   ISBN 978-981-15-2683-1 (eBook)
https://doi.org/10.1007/978-981-15-2683-1

This Springer imprint is published by the registered company Springer Nature Singapore Pte Ltd.
The registered company address is: 152 Beach Road, #21-01/04 Gateway East, Singapore 189721, Singapore

MELT

The Models *of* Engaged Learning and Teaching

Fluid, connected and sophisticated thinking, early childhood to Ph.D.

Preface

This book is about the Models of Engaged Learning and Teaching (or MELT for short), which fluidly connect to 100 years of educational research and 100,000 years of human learning and sophisticated thinking. The MELT are a family of models with an ancestry that shares common features and that necessarily evolve to fit new and emerging contexts. Because of their adaptability and shared features, the MELT have provided a way for teachers, academics, sessional and professional staff to bring together the years of education, from primary/elementary school education through to the middle years, high school, technical education, undergraduate, master's and doctoral study. This connection was evident, for example, when teachers, academics and professional staff from these contexts shared their adaptations and uses of the MELT at the International MELT conference in 2017 and especially through informal conversations about learning. Context-specific examples of MELT use are found throughout the book and associated website. The MELT may provide you with a way to deepen your understanding of the crucial role that you play in students' learning and where your work fits in the span of their educational experiences. Along with this insight, the MELT may also enable to you enhance the learning of students under your care.

These models, when used in concert, have helped teachers, academics, professional staff and especially students to make connections between different subjects and disciplines, from accounting to zoology, as well as transdisciplinary studies. Sophisticated thinking is not context-bound, but rather learned best in a variety of contexts, where connections between learning tasks may not be readily apparent but need to be made explicit not only to students but also to teachers in different contexts. The MELT also enable conversations between people with differing, sometimes polarised, educational philosophies—for example, between behaviourists employing Direct Instruction and social constructivists who employ discovery learning.

Polarised perspectives about learning were evident in my visit to a Pacific Island village community a few weeks ago. But the polarised perspectives I saw did not represent a tension but rather different points on a learning continuum, different ways through which students engaged in learning. Below, I recount that experience in a story called *Place Value*, which is set in two very different learning environments that existed in the village. In the first environment, there was a sense of fun and freedom for young children playing in a tree. In the other environment, an indoor classroom, the simplicity of the mathematical concept being presented belied the sophisticated thinking needed for the young children to learn the concept. This story is symbolic of the potential and tensions across formal education, representing as it does extremes in terms of students determining their own learning through play and involved in a teacher-directed lesson. These same tensions and potential are played out across formal and informal education and so the story sets the scene for you to grasp the breadth of learning and the breadth of the MELT.

Whatever your educational responsibility, as you read *Place Value*, consider this premise: the skills that the children demonstrated under the village tree and in the classroom are the same skills your students need and use on a daily basis, whether they are in primary/elementary school or conducting doctoral research. Regardless of educational level or subject area, good teaching always facilitates sophisticated thinking, but educational understanding strongly influences how and when this thinking is facilitated. Therefore this story is used in Chap. 2, along with stories from high school and university, to introduce the core characteristics of the MELT and illuminate connections of the MELT across years and contexts.

Place Value

While I swam in the ocean at the end of the tropical day, the children caught my attention as they played unsupervised under the spreading tree down by the shoreline. Their ages ranged from three to six years old. One child played with shells, one laid out a mat as if proffering items to sell, two were in different branches of the tree, one shook the branches, one just hung on, and two more were hidden from my view but darted into sight occasionally. Each seemed to occupy a separate world of play and exploration, of choosing what to do and where to do it. But despite these separate activities, all the children were within a radius of 6 metres, whether horizontally or vertically, and chattered in their mother tongue.

When I left the water at twilight, the children of the village who were over seven years old played volleyball on the sand and shell court, with an eight-year old officiating and making sure they adhered strictly to international rules.

The next day, I attended the Year 1/2 class in the primary school of the village and saw three of the children who had been playing in and under the tree the day before.

The children's play tree by the shore

A Pacific primary school in a village setting

The thirty-one children sat closely packed together on a Pacific Island *i-TaliTali* mat. The teacher began with some maths terminology and showed flash cards to the children.

Reading the card being held up by the teacher, Ms. Kristi, one child called out, 'Plus value'.

All the children chanted, 'Plus value, plus value'.

Ms. Kristi corrected '*Place value*', and the children chanted, 'place value, place value'.

Referring to the concept of numeral position in a two-digit number, Ms. Kristi asked the students, 'Is place value on your right or on your left?'

'Left', called some children.

Then eight children were selected to go to the front and each took a number from a box and held it to their chest for all to see. Numbers chosen were 9, 41, 11, 57, 5, 17, 20 and 29.

Ms. Kristi asked these eight children to arrange themselves in increasing numerical order. They began to shuffle, reorder, pause, look at each other's numbers and shuffle some more until they stood in a straight line in the sequence '5, 9, 11, 41, 17, 20, 29, 57'. Guided by their teacher, who pointed to each number in turn, the children on the mat read the numbers in order from their right to left: 'five, nine, eleven, fourteen...'.

Ms. Kristi paused at this number and began, 'For...' and one student completed 'Forty-one'.

Ms. Kristi paused thoughtfully. Then she said, 'Let's move on' and resumed pointing.

The children called out 'Forty-one... seventeen... twenty... twenty-nine... fifty-seven'.

'Is it correct or not?' asked Ms. Kristi.

The children called in unison, 'Not', so Ms. Kristi asked, 'which number is incorrect? Not in the proper place?'

One girl standing in the sequence and holding '5' pointed to the fourth student and said, 'forty-one'.

'How do you know that forty-one should not stand here?'

The student did not answer. No student answered.

'So this forty-one should go where?'

Many children pointed to the next position up, so the teacher prompted forty-one and seventeen to shuffle and change places.

The sequence became: 5, 9, 11, 17, **41**, 20, 29, 57.

'There. How do you know this forty-one should stand there?'

No answer.

Ms. Kristi continued, 'Any other number is in the wrong place?'

'Twenty-nine', a student called out.

'Twenty-nine should go where?'

'Besides seventeen', one student called out, and the student with twenty-nine shuffled there, passing forty-one.

5, 9, 11, 17, **29**, **41**, 20, 57

'Any other number?'

'No', called students in unison.

'Are you sure?'

'Twenty!' a boy called out.

'Right. Where should it go?'

'Besides seventeen'.

'Very good. Let's read the numbers together'.

'Five... nine... eleven... seventeen... twenty... twenty-nine... forty-one... fifty-seven'.

'Very good'. The children, Ms. Kristi and I all clapped.

In *Place Value* we have three children learning in two vastly different ways in two very different spaces. Under, in and near the tree, they were unsupervised, chose what to do and had their own sense of place. Their learning through play was in keeping with various forms of discovery learning, and in tune with social constructivist thinking. In the classroom, they followed prescribed instructions with an activity that ultimately had right or wrong answers and was placed culturally and physically on the Pacific Island mat, made through the weaving process called *i-Talitali*. The mathematics learning was in keeping with Direct Instruction, where students are primarily acquiring the canon of maths, fitting in with objectivist thinking. In both activities, there was evidence of highly sophisticated learning: in the classroom where the learning objectives were pre-determined by the teacher; and near the tree, with curiosity-driven learning and no thought to objectives or outcomes. Which form of learning is more important, more relevant or more enabling?

Your own answer to that question will say a lot about your educational philosophy. As far as the MELT are concerned, the answer is that both are valuable, relevant and mutually enabling. I hope some readers of this book are oriented to Direct Instruction and didactic learning, some align with discovery learning, that some are somewhere between, and some see the whole thing as a continuum. That's not to shift you from your position—I'm sure it is well considered and based on a good rationale. But when you talk to educators with other perspectives, you may find that the MELT enables you to have more sensible, more formative, more complementary conversations than you have had in the past, and that disconnected aspects of education may become more connected.

The MELT rationale is that all enduring educational theories and practices usefully inform education and when they connect as a complementary set, this will provide a richer learning environment for students. In *Place Value*, for example, the teacher was guiding the students towards specific, correct answers about numbers in a sequence. However, she did this in a Socratic fashion and elicited many responses and thoughts from students, some of whom were demonstrably constructing ideas individually or socially. Was the teacher correct to provide an approach which required students to engage in the construction of 'right-or-wrong' knowledge? From a purist theoretical perspective, this approach maybe counterproductive because of the clash between a constructivist paradigm and an objectivist one. For instance, from an objectivist perspective, if students constructed an incorrect understanding of place value, this would have negative implications for their enduring engagement with maths. From a constructivist perspective, if students were corrected on an answer that they volunteered in good faith, this could be counterproductive to their ongoing confidence and willingness to engage in learning. But from the pragmatic perspective of the MELT, a 'bricolage', a blending of what works, is not only possible, but desirable, providing that teachers understand what they are trying to achieve, how they will achieve it and especially know why this is their goal.

Learning that is structured in order to help students acquire mandated knowledge is not, by default, powerful, but neither is learning through play. One could argue that without guided teaching, students involved in play (such as the children in the tree) may merely be reproducing their cultural setting and knowledge, not learning to be critical thinkers. This would suggest that play can be more reproductive and less conceptually free than it appears on the surface. But Direct Instruction and learning through play *can* be powerful, and in the context of the MELT, the combination of these and other modes of learning provides a powerful incentive for students to learn to think in sophisticated ways.

Learning and teaching are complex, and individuals, groups and systems will see the same things differently through the MELT, as each will inhabit different social and cultural worlds. I offer the MELT as a way in which our educational worlds can become a little less polarised, and a little more connected and fluid across the years and contexts in order to improve student learning.

Adelaide, Australia   John Willison
November 2019

Acknowledgements

This book is dedicated to my daughter Nadia, an intrepid learner.

The cartoons that comprise the chapter title pages are drawn by Aaron Humphry.

All materials are under 4.0 Creative Commons licence to be shared, adapted and re-shared with attribution.

Joe Miller edited my often convoluted writing and proof read with his eagle eye.

Many colleagues and students have contributed in so many ways, and I greatly appreciate the feedback on drafts from Chad Habel, Chido Alozie, Chris Trevitt, Colin Sharp, Jasvir Kaur, Kara Loy, Lyn Torre, Nadia Willison, Penny Vervoost, Ray Tolhurst, Sheryl Mills, Sue Garvin and Suzanne Schibeci. Thanks to the blind reviewers who provided provocative insights that improved the book.

All the photos in the book were taken by the author, except the Fronticepiece Gold drop, which is from Shutterstock.com, under a non-exclusive right to use, modify and reproduce worldwide.

Contents

Acronyms

ATL	Approaches to Learning
CLT	Cognitive Load Theory
ECE	Early Childhood Education
IB	International Baccalaureate
MELT	Models of Engaged Learning and Teaching
OPS	Optimising Problem Solving
PBL	Problem Based Learning
RBL	Research Based Learning
RSD	Research Skill Development
STEM	Science, Technology, Engineering and Maths
writE	Writing and Reading Integrated with Talking about Experiments
WSD	Work Skill Development

Chapter 1:
What is our Purpose?
Embark & Clarify

Chapter 1
What Is Our Purpose?

1.1 Purpose

There are a lot of hidden similarities in education. Differences are often emphasised, and similarities hidden, by the articulation of context-specific terminology and techniques. These include differences associated with ways of learning and teaching, such as pedagogy versus andragogy; epistemological perspectives including objectivism versus constructivism; pedagogical approaches, for example, Direct Instruction versus discovery learning; disciplinary ways of speaking and doing such as counting and accounting versus zoo visits and zoology; and ways of researching, as evident in qualitative versus quantitative methods.

Between all of these perspectives and approaches are genuine differences that are good and helpful, for they mirror ways of learning, teaching and researching in a variety of contexts. Such differences in perspective and approach mirror the differences between the communities to which they belong. However, these perspectives and approaches also share quite a few similarities.

This book is about the similarities. The similarities are important because they can be the connective elements across formal education, for teachers, principals, academics, communities, education systems, parents and especially for learners. Frequently, education comes across to students one learning activity, one assignment, one subject at a time. But all those integrally involved aim for education to become a forest of learning for students, rather than a sequence of individual trees. That forest is a complex ecosystem of interactions, involving all year levels, all subjects and all educational concepts growing in health and harmony. Where all the individual parts join together into a complex whole is the location that students develop 21st century skills, becoming critical thinkers and problem solvers who are research-minded and information-savvy.

In order to connect the similarities so that students learn more effectively to solve complex problems, think critically, research and make evidence-based decisions, this book introduces and explains the Models of Engaged Learning and Teaching (MELT). The MELT provide an understanding of the connections between diverse

© The Author(s) 2020
J. Willison, *The Models of Engaged Learning and Teaching*,
SpringerBriefs in Education, https://doi.org/10.1007/978-981-15-2683-1_1

educational contexts, approaches, ideas and activities, and so enable a variety of different perspectives, practices and energies to work together. The MELT illuminate a way for educators and learners to participate in the development of sophisticated thinking skills, where the individual trees are more clearly connected in a forest of learning.

The purpose of this book, then, is to connect disparate energies and ideas of education through the MELT in order to facilitate students' development of sophisticated thinking. Educational theory and practice has tended towards conflict, creating uncertainties, distrust and wasted effort. With projections that Earth will reach a population of 8 billion people in 2023 [1], we need a new, more complementary style of education for the billion human brains that will be born from 2023 to 2030 [1], for they will become the leaders of the planet from 2040. Many of the problems they grapple with as leaders will be human-generated.

From Dewey in 1904/1974 [2] to Bundy in 2004 [3], 100 years of education research produced a set of understanding of learning as diverse as human learning and sophisticated thinking over the past 100,000 years. From MELT's perspective, this diversity is necessary, insightful and if not complete, then well-rounded, for informing education. As we move into an era where e-learning blended with face-to-face is the norm in schools, and in many technical education and university programmes, what do we need to know about human learning 100 Millennia ago, and how does it connect to the twenty-first Century?

The first 4 billion anatomically modern *Homo sapiens* born, from around 200 millennia ago [4, 5] to 100 millennia Before Present (BP) [6, 7] have a fossil record that demonstrates just a little innovation [8, 9]. Our large-brained ancestors primarily survived in the environments in which they were raised, or adapted to the new environments into which they moved.

The flurry of innovation shown in the archaeological record from around 100 millennia ago [8] onwards marks a transition to modern human behaviours. This set of behaviour is manifested in the development of diverse technologies, including hunting tools, fire control and chemical modifications, and abstract representations such as artworks. From this time, *Homo sapiens* are clearly apes with sophisticated thinking enabled by adaptive learning. Humans were not merely wandering into new environments from this time, but taking more calculated risks to get to new places, as evidenced by transport technologies such as simple canoes.

This flurry of innovation was self-perpetuating. One reason for this was that development compounded: one tool led to the development of another tool, and when both were used together, this enabled further development [9]. Another reason was that humans could now observe others' *intentional* adaptation of things, so that the *idea* of innovation became apparent. At some point in human history, someone first coined a word for the idea of intentional change, and humans armed with such a word may have caused the concept of innovation to reproduce like a meme [10], further accelerating innovative practice.

The innovation flurry was also driven by the fact that many of our innovative solutions became problems themselves. Enhanced hunting technologies at times led to the extinction of the prey on which humans depended. Domestication of herd animals provided a breeding ground for many killer diseases that resulted in large-scale human and animal suffering. Wide adoption of crops led to the extreme use of herbicides and insecticides, and the clearing of natural habitats. And technologies that closed the distance between people through online social engagement across the globe enabled cyber-abuse to enter people's bedrooms and addictive behaviours to control the tempo of modern relationships. Solutions produced fresh problems, each of which required increasingly sophisticated solutions of their own. Thus, we became the problem-solving ape [11], in part because we had to learn to solve the problems we made for ourselves and for the whole planet. As a species, we have a knack of solving problems with solutions that create new, more complex problems.

The MELT provide a way to gather together and connect educational ideas and energies in a way that may help us to break out of the vicious circle of our solutions that cause more problems. This is possible because, as noted, the MELT connect to 100,000 years of human learning and 100 years of educational research; with this diverse set of otherwise conflicting set of understanding, the MELT can enable an education that is broadly savvy of the influences on education. The MELT intentionally draw together and represent disparate views of education theory and practice, so as to capture the broad sweep of learning and teaching, including Direct Instruction to discovery learning; objectivist perspectives on learning through to social constructivist thought; primary/elementary school to Ph.D. studies; and accounting to zoology and interdisciplinary notions; The MELT then can be used as a conceptual set to connect those with different roles such as caregivers, lab managers, learning advisors, learning designers, lecturers, librarians, principals, professors, parents, programme coordinators, sessional staff, supervisors of higher degree by research, teachers, vice chancellors and, crucially, students from primary/elementary school to Ph.D.

MELT is frequently put into action to help students understand their own sophisticated thinking and see more clearly the purpose for their own education that necessarily revolves around the further development of that thinking. It is not easy for teachers to have or develop a sense of purpose for students that goes beyond the immediacy of daily lessons to the big picture. For both students and teachers, MELT may be used as a thinking routine [12] that becomes habitual (but not mundane) and which, through repeated exposure, prompts growth in sophisticated thinking, not only about what to do and how to do it, but also metacognitive awareness.

When considering the last 100 years of educational research, our understandings of learning and teaching can seem more disparate than ever, and theory has not connected well with practice. For example, it is common for teachers to omit the explicit use of theoretical frameworks for their lesson planning and when leading other teachers [13]. However, we are also at a point of knowing an amazing amount about the complexities of teaching and learning. The MELT were formulated not to be theoretically pure, but through a consideration of major aspects of educational research and simultaneous reflection on classroom practice [14], as discussed in Chaps. 2 and 4. The models provide a conceptual framework for action, not a theory or set of theories. A 'conceptual framework' pertains here to a structure that guides thinking, that sets the parameters for considering learning and teaching.

The MELT provide a practical philosophy, then, connecting theories with theories and practices with practices, and especially connecting theory with practice. The MELT makes the skills associated with sophisticated thinking explicit, with the intention of encouraging coherent, explicit and cyclic development of such thinking across students' education.

This book spans early childhood education (ECE) to postgraduate study and contains examples across those contexts. But why would an early childhood teacher care about Master's level study, or undergraduate or high school? Why would a Ph.D. supervisor care about primary school learning? I suggest a reason is that the MELT can help with the connections across education, ultimately improving learning and teaching in ECE, primary and secondary school, technical education, undergraduate, master's, Ph.D. and employment contexts. Another reason is that all students use and teachers value the skills and attitudes associated with the MELT, because the models encapsulate what we do when we engage in sophisticated thinking [14].

A brief history of MELT

Beginning in 2004, my colleague Kerry O'Regan and I synthesised disparate literature and reflections on classroom practice, culminating in the first fully-developed version of the MELT, called the Research Skill Development (RSD) framework [15]. The RSD was employed in two national studies [15–17], which were designed to determine its efficacy in higher education contexts. However, the word 'research' did not always connect to people's practice. For example, Sue Bandaranaike coordinated student placements in industry called Work Integrated Learning or Cooperative Education and knew that 'research' did not fit her context. In 2009, Sue re-articulated the sophisticated thinking expressed in the RSD in terminology that was true to employment contexts, producing the Work Skill Development (WSD) framework [18]. Then, in quick succession, colleagues in Oral Health developed the Clinical Reflection Framework in 2012 [19], student-tutors developed a pentagon-shaped version for engineering, called the Optimising Problem-Solving pentagon [20] and an early childhood music teacher developed a song version called 'Research Mountain' [21], both in 2014. Colleagues from the University of the South Pacific developed a process-based version [22], using the metaphor of weaving a Pacific Island mat, the *italitali* mat that students were sitting on in *Place Value*. In 2018 Monash University developed the Digital Skills Development (DSD) framework [23] and in 2019 the Blended and Engaged Learning Zones (BELZ) [24] was devised for the design and evaluation of modes that are explicitly blended with e-learning. (Note that 'learning' is used preferentially to 'e-learning' in this book because modern learning is so often bound up with, or mediated fully by, the electronic that it is often not helpful to differentiate [25]).

By 2016, the number of RSD-based models had grown to such an extent that one name was chosen to be emblematic of the characteristics and purpose of all of them: the Models of Engaged Learning and Teaching [15]. It took from 2004 to 2016 to determine the core characteristics of these models, and to find a name that could connect them conceptually. The MELT evolved over time to become a set of related, but context-specific, representations of how sophisticated thinking could be taught and learned, in keeping with *Homo sapiens*' history [9] and contemporary learning environments [14, 15].

Contemporary issues

By unpacking the MELT, this book will address four perennial, yet contemporary, issues:

- How educators may effectively help students think in sophisticated ways, including understanding their own thinking processes. Sophisticated thinking takes many forms, and includes researching, problem-solving, evidence-based practice, clinical reasoning, ethical reasoning, critical thinking, discovering, inquiring and understanding concepts, as well as metacognition.
- How to connect different aspects of education so that they mutually reinforce and complement each other:

  - Across students' education, from early childhood through to school completion, technical and further education, undergraduate, master's and Ph.D. level, onto employment and continuing professional development.
  - Across subjects and disciplines from counting and accounting to zoo visits and zoology, multidisciplinary, interdisciplinary and transdisciplinary learning.
  - Between sometimes competing paradigms, theories and teaching practices.

- How to deepen educators' understanding of the dimensions and practicalities of student autonomy in learning. This understanding will illuminate connections between disparate discourses around student-centred learning, Direct Instruction, Cognitive Load Theory, Threshold Concepts, discovery learning and networked learning, as well as student cultural, language and learning diversity.
- How educators can effectively engage with educational theory in ways that offer practical value for teaching and learning environments.

The book introduces the MELT as a way to conceptualise how such enabling, connecting, deepening and engaging may take place.

This chapter details the purpose and features of the book and of its namesake subject, the Models of Engaged Learning and Teaching. Section 1.2 outlines the MELT's six *facets* of sophisticated thinking, elaborated along a *continuum of learning autonomy*. Section 1.3, called *Parachute*, comprises a story about two students, Shelly and Katie, each engaged in an individual short project in the first year of high school. As well as covering some of the types of learning that are common across formal education and in many different disciplinary and interdisciplinary contexts, this story is true to the sophisticated learning that humans have engaged in for 100,000 years. In Sect. 1.4, *100 billion brains*, humans are contrasted with beavers, who were the premier engineers of the past 20 million years, but who were stuck in their mode of learning. Unlike beavers, humans have developed multiple ways of learning, suggesting that a multiplicity of teaching strategies are not just possible but desirable. Section 1.5, *One billion brains more*, outlines the absolute need to develop sophisticated thinking in order to address educational and planet-wide problems, requiring a conceptualisation like MELT to connect different teaching approaches and ideas.

Section 1.6 provides the structure of this book, where each chapter's title is one of the seven questions that are central to each MELT *facet* and to *learning autonomy*. The chapter concludes with Sect. 1.7, *Student learning that resonates*. For the MELT, recognising and fostering a diverse range of teaching and learning strategies is absolutely central to effective education. Therefore, this book explicitly articulates the connections between disparate educational ideas, placing them all on the same *learning autonomy continuum* of the MELT, in the hope that these ideas will be taken together as a set and become more mutually supportive.

1.2 MELT Components

The MELT comprise the six *facets* of sophisticated thinking elaborated along a continuum of *learning autonomy*.

1.2.1 MELT Facets

The *facets* of the MELT concern the 'what' of learning and teaching. Content varies subject-by-subject, lesson-by-lesson and in the MELT focus, the 'what' concerns the skills and attitudes of sophisticated thinking as applied to, and mediated by, the content.

Figure 1.1 shows a version of the MELT that was inspired by engineering students who tutored in a large first year course. The student/tutors adapted MELT and devised a version that they called the Optimising Problem-Solving (OPS) pentagon. That version stripped out a lot of detail, resulting in a representation that is student friendly and focuses on the facets, rather than explicating *learning autonomy* directly to the students. Context-specific adaptations of MELT, portrayed in the pentagon configuration, are used, with students from Year 4 of primary school to master's level, and in introductions of MELT to educators in schools and universities.

Complex learning from ECE to Ph.D. always requires something akin to the six MELT *facets*. In many ways, these facets are clear and uncontroversial in nature if not in name, and commonly made explicit in education. Each MELT facet comprises a name made of verb couplets, an associated affective adjective, and a corresponding question, as shown in Table 1.1 (as well as a description, provided in Chap. 2).

The facets of MELT are quintessential processes whose descriptions act as triggers and connectors. As quintessential processes, the MELT facets can't independently capture the meaning for every context. They are fully dependent on the educators who adopt them, each of whom knows or is coming to know, what needs to happen in any learning situation that they are facilitating, and how to articulate the processes they are facilitating.

Each facet of the MELT is designed to 'trigger' words and phrases that better describe the facet's concepts in a particular context. These words and phrases then

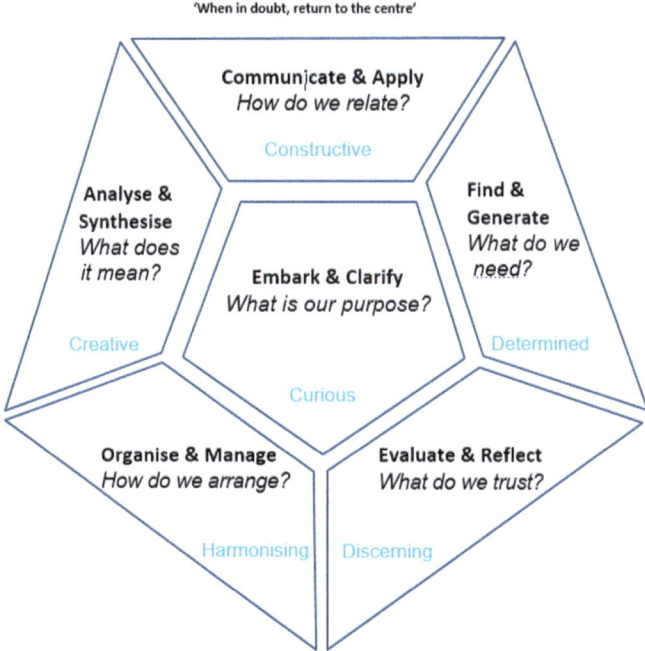

Fig. 1.1 The MELT Pentagon's six facets, each with a pair of verbs, a key question and an adjective in blue which represents the affective domain

Table 1.1 The six facets of MELT

Facet name (learning process)	Affective adjective	Question
Embark & clarify	Curious	What is our purpose?
Find & generate	Determined	What will we use?
Evaluate & reflect	Discerning	What do we trust?
Organise & manage	Harmonising	How do we arrange?
Analyse & synthesise	Creative	What does it mean?
Communicate & apply	Constructive	How do we relate?

may conceptually connect to other contexts which use different words and phrases for the same concepts being triggered by the facet. Without this conceptual connection, the processes associated with the same facet may otherwise seem unrelated to students and educators. For example, the facet *embark and clarify* may trigger terms that suit the start of a process such as 'pose research question', 'define problem' or 'determine need', depending on the terminology of the context and the purpose at hand. These terms do have useful differences, but they also have conceptual overlap that is frequently overlooked. As triggers, the facets are not generic skills, because 'generic' implies skills that students maybe able to generalise from one context to another. The facets may be better thought of as 'connectable skills' rather than transferable skills.

As an educational trigger, each facet has four vital inter-related components. Three are introduced above (verb couplets, affective adjective, key question), and the fourth component, introduced in Chap. 2, is a sentence description of each facet. Some educators may focus on the cognitive aspect (e.g., *embark*), some on the affective (e.g., *curious*), some on the question (what is our purpose?), some on all three. But together, these aspects provide the sense of what we are after across education, and that sense can be explicitly connected from one context to another. Subject and discipline-mediated ways of understanding and representing the facets vary widely [16–19], as demonstrated in Chap. 3's look at MELT use in a variety of contexts.

1.2.2   Continuum of Learning Autonomy

The *continuum of learning autonomy* in MELT concerns the 'how' of learning and teaching, that is, the ways that the facets maybe developed, making the continuum an explicit articulation of the teaching process for scaffolding the development of sophisticated thinking. It is also possible to enable students to understand their engagement in the learning process, and representation of the *continuum of learning autonomy* expressly for students is shown in Fig. 1.2. In the figure, the red pentagon represents lower levels of learning autonomy, where students *emulate*; a yellow pentagon at mid-levels of learning autonomy, where students *improvise*, and a blue pentagon representing high levels of learning autonomy, where students *initiate*. Students may emulate, then improvise, then initiate sophisticated learning and then proceed to emulate once more, for example, if the learning context shifts so that students are unfamiliar with new content, if conceptual demand goes up or as the expected rigour increases. In other words, *learning autonomy* in MELT is not unidirectional towards high autonomy, but rather shuttles back and forth, according to the young child's or the Ph.D. student's learning needs [27].

Learning autonomy in MELT maybe engineered by teachers, and matrix versions of MELT often articulate a five-level, teaching-oriented *continuum of learning autonomy*, shown in Fig. 1.3. Five levels of differentiation are sometimes helpful for teachers, whereas three levels are typically enough for students.

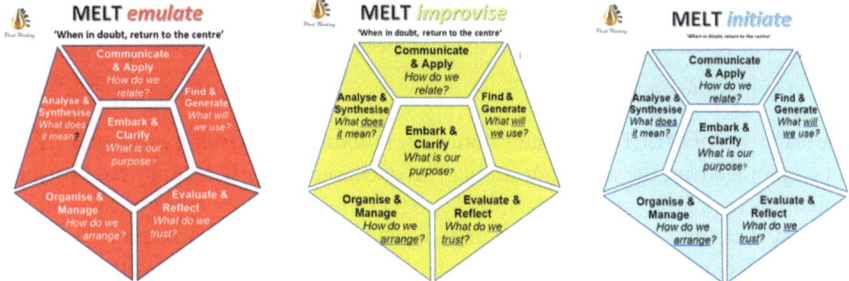

Fig. 1.2 A student-oriented *continuum of learning autonomy*, here represented by three verbs and corresponding colours: *emulate*, red; *improvise*, yellow; and *initiate*, blue (see www.rsd.edu.au/framework)

Models of Engaged Learning and Teaching

Continuum of Learning Autonomy

	Prescribed Research	Bounded Research	Scaffolded Research	Open-ended Research	Unbounded Research
Embark & Clarify *What is our purpose?*					
Find & Generate *What will we use?*					
Evaluate & Reflect *What do we trust?*					
Organise & Manage *How do we arrange?*					
Analyse & Synthesise *What does it mean?*					
Communicate & Apply *How do we relate?*					

Fig. 1.3 A teaching-oriented *continuum of learning autonomy*, here represented by five verbs and corresponding colours: *prescribed*, red; *bounded, orange; scaffolded*, yellow; *open-ended*, green; and *unbounded*, blue (details removed: see www.rsd.edu.au/framework)

Frequently, considerations regarding the extent of *learning autonomy* are left buried below the level of teachers' and students' consciousness. However, implicit understandings of *learning autonomy* permeate classrooms and supervision contexts in which teachers seek to develop sophisticated thinking [27]. The question below, associated with the *continuum of learning autonomy*, is arguably the most pressing concern in education, whether for face-to-face, online, augmented, virtual or blended realities. It is ultimately the most contentious question and because of this has the potential to connect disparate ideas in education:

How much guidance?

The six *facets* of MELT elaborated along the *continuum of learning autonomy* frame, but cannot answer, the above question. The question can only be answered by individual teachers and their students, by school communities, by systems and, maybe soon, by Teaching Machines (see Chap. 5) who understand the context of learning. The MELT explication of the *continuum of learning autonomy* provokes answers, however, around a healthy shuttling where students emulate, improvise and initiate and then proceed once more to emulate. The amount of guidance depends on the relationship of the student to what is learned, to the teacher and to the broader context, and the complexity of such relationship is best discussed and debated.

1.2.3 MELT as a Thinking Routine

Sharing the inter-relationships of facets and learning autonomy, the MELT takes on many forms and may be revisited in different guises along a student's learning journey. Some forms include tables with text, pentagon or jig-saw shapes, songs with actions, and a weaving metaphor; diverse MELT models are presented in Chap. 3. Formats and phrasings depend on the purpose chosen for each of the MELT, the intended audience, and educators' professional judgement, and so the MELT are necessarily fluid. With a growing number of emerging MELT, the models show the potential of working together as a set that conceptually connects the disparate ideas and energies of education. Multiple manifestations and uses of the same overarching framework by many educators, researchers and parents may, over time, richly develop the sophisticated thinking that enables students to create solutions to problems—solutions that do not become the cause of further problems.

Providing students with multiple exposures to MELT in many guises enables the six facets to become a *thinking routine* [12], a way of thinking that can conceptually accompany them throughout their education and remain afterwards. Researchers found that a hallmark of effective teachers was that they frequently employed explicit thinking strategies for students to use [11]. Teachers repeatedly introduced, modelled and used these strategies to facilitate student learning. The researchers called these *thinking routines* because they became almost second nature for students, and they were a vital component of 'making thinking visible' to teachers, parents and to the students themselves. The six facets of the MELT can become for students a *thinking routine* if teachers facilitate their use repeatedly. One final-year university student, looking back over multiple semesters of MELT use said 'because they have been consistently applying this structure to all of our assignments, we have *come to think that way for science*' [28]. MELT became a thinking routine for that student.

*Educ*ation connotes a process of *educ*ing, a 'leading out' of what is inside students, their capacities for sophisticated thinking, whereas the facilitation of learning content knowledge could be called *induc*ation. A combination of inducation and education provides the opportunity for sophisticated thinking to be nurtured in a content-rich environment. Students who employ skills in inquiry learning without much background knowledge and understanding often struggle [29], while an emphasis on content is frequently demotivational [30]. Diversity of pedagogies, teaching personalities and contexts, with inducational and educational elements, will provide rich learning. For example, it seems counterproductive to teach students to think critically while only presenting them with one understanding of critical thinking. Critical thinking in English literature looks quite different from critical thinking in astrophysics; students will develop richer, more robust and useful forms of critical thinking if presented with the diverse approaches and methods afforded by different subjects and disciplines and they can see the similarities and connections, not just the differences.

This book seeks connections, not through terminology or definitions, but by provoking thought on how sophisticated thinking maybe facilitated by MELT adaptation and use in many content-rich contexts. The book introduces, mirrors and represents MELT by using the seven questions above for its structure.

The story below, along with *Place Value* (Preface) and *Silver Fluoride* (Chap. 2) will be used in Chap. 2 to show how the complexities of sophisticated thinking are, across formal education, legitimately and usefully captured in MELT.

1.3 Parachute

This chapter emphasises purpose, and purpose is the underpinning theme in the classroom story below, called *Parachute*. A big range of teaching and learning strategies is evident in *Parachute*: there is a teacher present, a person who holds a vast amount of culturally-specific knowledge and who is keen to incorporate that into the students' own knowledge bases. The teacher has an intention for the learning that may or may not be realised student-by-student. There is a learner, Shelly, who is willing to take a risk and *innovate*, and another learner, Katie, who plays it safe and *emulates* the teacher. There are unnamed students who strongly influence the learning dynamic, even though the focus of the class is nominally an individual project.

This diversity of actors and actions is true to the reality of human learning across millennia, where the capacity to learn was a huge determinant of the survival and evolutionary direction of the species. At times in our prehistory, imitation and rote learning, forms of emulation, were far more effective for survival than discovery learning requiring innovation. However, there have also been many times where existing knowledge and practice were insufficient and, like Shelly below, individuals or groups needed to take risks and innovate. Without such adaptations, human groups would have perished or been overrun. Or they just may have missed an amazing opportunity unless they adapted and took risks, as demonstrated by the Polynesians who sailed into the unknown Pacific about 3,000 years ago [31].

Sophisticated thinking has always involved drawing on existing knowledge, evaluating that knowledge and then seeing if different knowledge and skills are needed. Like this book more broadly, *Parachute* does not romanticise discovery learning as a panacea, but neither does it promote a strong didactic approach as the solution. MELT is suggestive of something more fluid, something that takes shape and then flows again between didactic and discovery approaches. The story is narrated by me as a participant observer conducting research in Mrs. Breen's Year 8 science class [32], and shows the potential and problems with content knowledge acquisition and with discovery learning.

Parachute

'Continue on with your steps for your parachute,' calls Mrs. Breen, addressing the class during the double period before lunch. 'Then draw up an observation table. We have material in plastic bags, cotton, string of two different lengths, thick and thin.'

Shelly takes a compass and attempts to draw a circle on some plastic, using a pen. Once Shelly has cut out a misshapen circle, her desk partner Katie uses it as a template for her own experiment, cutting out a circle of plastic and a circle of cotton.

Shelly works on some calculations for a while, then comes up to me and says, 'I don't have enough plastic.'

She explains that her intention is to make a square parachute of the same area as the round one. I am shocked when I see how much plastic Shelly has left. There seems to be enough to make ten square parachutes of the same area as the round one she is holding.

'I need a square one hundred and eight by one hundred and eight centimetres,' she informs me.

My mind reels at the size of this square. It would have a surface area greater than her work desk, and yet is supposed to be the same area as the circle she has cut, a circle only a little larger than her open hand.

'Show me how you worked out the area,' I ask, wanting to find out how she could make such a miscalculation.

To find the area of the circle she has made, Shelly puts pi r squared into action, and her calculator reads '433.5'. So far, so good. Then, to find the length of a side of the square to make it an equivalent area, she hits the division button, followed by the four buttons.

'One hundred and eight,' she exclaims. 'See? It doesn't fit.'

Sure enough, her sheet of plastic would be dwarfed by a square with sides of 108 cm and, therefore, she thinks she doesn't have enough material.

I brace myself, remembering that Shelly is a very bright student and begin, 'The area of the circle is right, but the square is much too large. You just found the length of the side if 433.5 was the perimeter.'

'I don't know how to do it,' she says, looking up at the clock.

'What is the area of a square with sides of two centimetres?' I ask in Socratic fashion.

'Four centimetres squared,' Shelly answers.

'What are the sides of a square sized nine centimetres?'

'Three?'

'What did you do to get it?'

'Divide by itself?' asks Shelly in answer.

'Sort of,' I respond, thinking she is getting close.

'Find what and what... like square roo... like you..?'

I write '$\sqrt{9}$'.

'I don't know how to do that,' Shelly laments.

I show her the symbol on her calculator. It is term three of Year 8 and Shelly is in the top mathematics class. She says that does not know how to find the length of the sides of a square when given an area. She says that she does not know how to find the square root of a number, even using a calculator.

Much worse to me, though, is that she never thought for a second that there could be something wrong with the size of the square she had calculated. And she was an 'A' grade student in maths.

Shelly finds the square root to be 20.5, runs to her desk and immediately starts to rule up the plastic. There is now plenty of material to make a square parachute with sides of 20.5 centimetres.

Mrs. Breen goes to the doorway to speak to a number of students dropping parachutes outside: 'Alright everyone, back in.'

As Shelly hears this, she says, 'Shivers,' quietly to herself, grabs both parachutes and heads for the door.

She almost makes it outside, when Mrs. Breen waves everyone back to their seats. 'I want everyone to listen.'

Back at her seat, Shelly works hastily to make sure her parachutes are ready to test.

'I know most of you have done the experiment...' (Shelly works at a more frenzied pace) '...but I also want you to do a bar graph.'

Mrs. Breen draws an example on the board.

Katie begins to do some test drops with her two parachutes. She is comparing the drop time of a cloth parachute and a plastic parachute, which was the example provided by Mrs. Breen. Both parachutes float to earth in a satisfying parachute-like manner.

Shelly grabs the stop-watch and starts to drop her square parachute. However, the string pulls off the plastic.

'Mine doesn't work. It's crap,' she sulks to Katie.

Shelly quickly repairs the square parachute and drops it again (Fig. 1.4).

In the results table, under the column heading 'round', Shelly writes '0.68', then crosses it out. Next to this, she writes '1.12' after another drop. Then, she crosses this out. She drops again and writes '0.93', yet changes the nine to a six, so her only number in that column reads '0.63'. This dropping, erasing and writing process continues for several minutes.

Mrs. Breen passes and asks, 'So what happened? Is it OK?'

'Yep', says Shelly, 'the round one takes longer to hit the ground.'

'Did you use several measurements?'

'Yes.'

Fig. 1.4 Shelly determines the drop time for a square, plastic parachute

Mrs. Breen smiles, extremely pleased with Shelly's success.

Mrs. Breen returns to the front and explains to the whole class, 'In the conclusion, list what went wrong, and how you could improve.'

Shelly gets to work on the conclusion of her report. She writes, 'If the key factors are the same the parachutes should come down at the same rate as it was not proven here I have come to the conclusion that the shape does matter to the time.'

Katie works on improving her cloth parachute. She drops it and coos, 'Cool,' as she watches its smooth flight.

As it floats gently to earth once more, she says abstractly, 'I hate maths with a passion.'

Shelly echoes her sentiment: 'I hate maths too.'

1.3.1 **MELT Features in *Parachute***

In *Parachute*, Shelly and Katie were engaged in learning that involved designing experiments and determining independent variables, dependent variables and controlled variables. MELT is one way of representing the sophisticated thinking in this story. The simple analysis of *Parachute* below foreshadows the six facets of MELT that are introduced more thoroughly in Chap. 2.

Shelly is determined to compare square and round parachutes, whereas Katie looked at cotton versus plastic, the teacher's example. This is where each decided what to *embark* on for their experiment, as well as beginning the complex process of ongoing *clarification* of purpose.

Early on, Shelly worked to craft two plastic parachutes of different shape but the same size, and realised that she needed to use geometry to achieve this. She created the round parachute, measured it and generated its surface area from pi r squared. Then she used the formula for perimeters of a square to calculate its sides—generating a number that dwarfed the circle. Shelly *found* needed resources (plastic, a calculator and maths formulas from memory) and *generated* data using an empirical methodology.

Shelly realised there was a problem, and her *evaluation* correctly suggested that there was insufficient material to make a square big enough to match her calculation. I was surprised that she did not notice the huge discrepancy in size between her actual circle and her proposed square. It seems she implicitly trusted the mathematical calculation, even when the discrepancy was huge, evidencing little *reflection* at that point. Shelly sought help from me for more materials. However, instead of sourcing more, I prompted her to consider that her calculation of the size of the square was wrong. At this point, Shelly and I tried to determine whether she knew an appropriate formula to determine the amount of material she would need for a square parachute. When she struggled remembering a correct equation for the area of a square, I provided her numerous cues until I virtually told her area equals the length of one side squared.

Once she applied a formula that gave a more sensible answer, she produced a square parachute of comparable size to the round one, and began to time parachute drops. She wrote, erased and rewrote results into her results table. This *organisation* of results was accompanied by the *evaluation* of data as somehow wrong and in need of re-recording. All the while, Shelly had the huge pressure of *managing* her dwindling time to set up the entire experiment, which was novel, in that no one else was contrasting shape, while others were following the teacher's example procedure.

Shelly *analysed* her data and found that the round one took longer to fall. Her *synthesis* was the overall finding that 'shape does matter to drop time, given the same surface area'.

Throughout, Shelly listened to and talked with her desk partner, me and the teacher, while she also wrote and recorded, demonstrating multiple modes of *communication*. She *applied* remembered and prompted knowledge (formulas for the area of a circle and of a square) to the experiment, as well as her evolving knowledge of experimental design, relating this to her existing knowledge and to others in the classroom.

The story is set in a school science laboratory, but Shelly engaged in sophisticated thinking that is as relevant to hunter-gatherers as it is to learners in virtual worlds. Lab learning, hunting and online gaming differ in many ways and the fundamental neuronal wiring of the brains of children brought up engaging heavily online maybe quite different to that of hunter-gatherers. However, the story contains elements of the sophisticated thinking that we crave as teachers and such thinking spans 100,000 years. Like most learners throughout human prehistory and history, Shelly experienced frustrations, setbacks and unresolved tensions, as well as some successes.

The in-class learning of Shelly, involving exploring and risk taking, and of Katie, involving emulating and safety, demonstrated a lot of the potential and pitfalls connected to *learning autonomy*. Shelly attempted to work on her own questions about square and round parachutes, showing much more autonomy in learning than Katie and others in the class by *initiating* in many MELT facets, and *improvising* in the rest. Katie was primarily *emulating* the teacher's example. Thus, there were differentiated experiences along the continuum of *learning autonomy* in the same room, at the same time, given the same parameters by the teacher. The task in *Parachute* had the scope of *open-ended inquiry*, but because the teacher provided modelling that students were permitted to imitate, most students took the safer, easier way of emulating.

Shelly's higher autonomy had associated risks, exemplified by her extreme miscalculation. Shelly had possibly applied the formula for the area of a square dozens of times in her schooling, and this time she was way off any sensible number. While there is potential for huge learning here, the situation is also an example of a huge learning curve. Where that curve is too steep, some students may experience enough demotivation and discouragement to put them off trying. However, Shelly was not deterred by her miscalculation, in part because she did not perceive the discrepancy in the actual size of the round parachute and the calculated size of the square one. Instead of recalculating, she sought more material to match her calculation. From a Problem Based Learning (PBL) perspective, if Shelly recognised the discrepancy between calculation and size, this could have led to deep learning [32]. However, within the constraints of the classroom, she had little time to complete and submit her work. Practicalities of teaching, such as lesson length, frequently dictate what actually happens in formal education regardless of theory informing the lesson. Ultimately, Shelly demonstrated in the eighty minutes before lunch the sophisticated thinking that comprises MELT's six *facets* on the higher end of the *continuum of learning autonomy*. Often these *facets* are not deployed consciously and, much like an unopened parachute, learners may have a hard landing when conceptual difficulties emerge.

In *Parachute*, Shelly's own research question created a need for mathematical calculation and specific mathematical equations. This maybe contrasted with *Place Value*, where children required no specific knowledge to play around the tree, and in their classroom, the focus was on content knowledge inculcation or construction. Shelly, a student of thirteen, had experienced seven years of schooling in maths, and it's reasonable to assume that she would have learned about calculating the area of a square several years earlier. *Place Value* represented learning experiences in two different contexts and each elicited a very different *learning autonomy*. However, *Parachute* showed some of the tensions that maybe evident within a single context, and highlighted the intimate connection between content knowledge and inquiry learning. This tension between an appropriate knowledge base and learning through discovery has been evident throughout human prehistory. The questions of engaged learning and teaching are as pertinent to ancient *Homo sapiens* as they are to contemporary humans whether they are inhabiting real or virtual environments. The wiring of our brains may be or become quite different, but the questions of learning are the same.

Through our prehistory, humans proved to be highly adaptable because our brains were not programmed to 'get stuck' on one mode of learning. But ironically for a discipline centred on learning, the practice and research of formal education have tended to become 'stuck'. That is, researchers have often prioritised researching the forms of learning that seem optimal to them, and looking at the learning gains by contrasting performance, e.g., that of Direct Instruction versus discovery learning. The findings of studies, of course, have always depended on what was valued as a learning gain in the measurements. But a mentality which emphasises measurement has possibly diminished educators' awareness of the potential range of ways to learn, with a whole spectrum of possibilities being minimised for the sake of theory and parsimony. Search for a grand theory that underpins all learning undermines the potential of humankind to engage in diverse and enriching learning and teaching. To maximise the efforts of educators and students, it is necessary to pull together the disparate threads in education, in a way that reflects how humans were geared to learn 100,000 years ago and how they are currently geared to learn. In educational practice and theory, MELT connotes a fluidity, rather than being stuck in one place, in keeping with our learning as a species.

1.4 100 Billion Brains: Learning from Human Prehistory to Contemporary Classrooms and Learning Environments

Humans are the only known animals to use systematic, descriptive labels for living things, including ourselves. And while we labelled our cousins with systematic and descriptive species names such as *Homo erectus* and *Homo habitus*, we chose for ourselves the more interpretive title of *Homo sapiens*, or 'wise man'. If sentient animals had a vote, would they describe modern humans as wise? We are certainly a learning animal, but many animals are that too. What about our learning is distinctively *sapiens*? We have big brains, proportionally, but Neanderthals had a bigger brain volume [33] and still died out.

As noted early in this chapter, *Homo sapiens* have been very efficient at solving problems whose solutions created new problems which emerged days, years or centuries later. This is highly disturbing, albeit probably inevitable. The disturbing side of the process whereby solutions beget problems is obvious, with rates of species extinction unprecedented since the meteor that led to the demise of the dinosaurs, degradation of water, air, soils and society, and massive migrations, alienations and competition between cultures, religions, political ideologies and nations.

The inevitable side of the process by which human-made solutions generate new problems may come as a surprise. To demonstrate this inevitability, I present a comparison between humans and beavers—the pre-eminent engineers of the animal world, for more than 20 million years [34] up until 12,000 years ago. The reason for this comparison is that those early engineer-beavers were more instinctive than purposively engaged in their learning, whereas humans frequently need engaged teaching to enable engaged learning.

1.4.1 Beaver and Human Know-How

The massive engineering projects requiring complex social behaviour, up until relatively recently in the earth's history, were conducted by beavers. It is only in the recent past, starting about 12,000 years ago [35], that human engineering projects were conducted on a scale more massive than beavers' dams, even though the human physique's capacity for engineering has exceeded the beavers' physical capacity for 200,000 years.

So, how is it that beavers were more able to conduct massive engineering projects than humans for over 180,000 years? In short, because it took a whole lot of learning about materials, physics, chemistry, maths, nature, and ourselves, including through artistic expression, creative imagining and philosophising, for humans to take top spot on massive-scale engineering. Critically, what is important to, and reflective of, MELT, is that this human learning was diverse in mode.

A curious feature of beaver dam-building know-how is that the majority of it is in their genes [36, 37]. Beavers can learn over time to build better dams, but their fundamental damming behaviour is hard-wired. So, even if you could challenge a beaver to build some other massive structure (such as a bridge) it would not have the cognitive capacity to do so. Beavers are smooth-brained (lissencephalic) whereas humans and other apes have wormy brains featuring gyri and sulci, which allow for more neurons and synapses to be packed into the same space. Pre-programed know-how only gets you so far, and beavers can't generalise their learning from dams to other engineering projects.

As with beavers, *Homo sapiens* have genetically programmed know-how: we can suck, chew and crawl, and maybe some humans can walk and run without examples. But we can't talk, write, read or do anything like build a dam without learning to do so, whether by watching and listening, with a teacher or through trial and error. Beavers' engineering knowledge is pre-packaged, whereas ours developed over the course of tens of thousands of years, and needs to be culturally transmitted rather than genetically transmitted.

Perhaps because we have so little genetic know-how, human babies are called 'sponges', as they appear ready to soak up and imitate almost anything they see and hear. As a tragic example, orphans in Romania who were deprived of care by adults [38] mimicked the movements of cranes that they could see through the window. Engaged learning is the norm for a baby in three modes: being taught, observing, and experimenting through trial and error. All these three modes are vital for normal development, and the second and last are ubiquitous for babies.

Being taught, however, requires someone to facilitate the learning. This could involve correcting a child's pronunciation, instructing on the number of protons in magnesium or suggesting a strategy for brush strokes on a painting. While common, teaching and being taught are not ubiquitous. This is the most difficult to operationalise of the three modes mentioned above, because it depends on the intentionality of someone who is not the learner. Such intentionality requires some effort, some thought. In societies with universal schooling, the process of teaching and being taught entails effort by the whole of society. So this book is about engaged teachers. And because learning can and does take place independently of a teacher, this book is also about engaged learners. Most of all, it is about the relationship of engaged learners and engaged teachers together, where sometimes the teachers learn and sometimes the learners teach.

MELT frame a range of teaching pedagogies that fit human learning. At one extreme end of a teaching spectrum, beavers don't need pedagogy; for them, there is little intentional teaching and little capacity to engage in it. At the other end, humans need a multiplicity of pedagogies that represent our broad-ranged sophisticated thinking, and the MELT represents this range. The use of the plural word 'models' in MELT is intended to capture the numerous ways of conceptualising engaged learning and teaching. The broad parameters that all existing and future MELT share attempt to capture the breadth of education research, theorising and practice for the past 100 years, and the breadth of the human experience of learning and teaching for the past 100,000 years.

'Engagement', the 'E' in MELT, is a term sometimes used glibly in education, but in MELT it is used deliberately to suggest the same idea that it connotes in the context of a manual car: it won't move unless you engage the clutch. There must be cognitive meshing. Learning, then, is a 'moving forward' into a place we have not yet been conceptually, enabled by engagement. Teaching is driving towards a goal, a forward impetus where frequently the teacher steers. But in contemporary classrooms, online environments, and throughout human prehistory, learners may be the ones steering and controlling the accelerator and brake. Teaching, in MELT, is attending to and establishing the preconditions and conditions for learning, including cognitive, affective and social aspects. Without a teacher, planned learning is difficult. However, when the learning is driven by a teacher, it is never guaranteed to be positive or effective, especially if students are demotivated about the learning at hand. It is a huge challenge to teach a class of students effectively day after day, to tutor, to supervise, and to nurture learning.

1.4.2 Inevitable Earth: Problems with Dams

Another good reason to know about beaver learning is to deepen our understanding of human learning and its consequences. As beavers evolved increasing capacity, physically and cognitively, to build dams, they not only built bigger and better dams, but they changed entire ecosystems through the flooding of valleys to make lakes. They changed the course of evolution for untold species of plants, animals, fungi and bacteria. However, this process took millions of years, and entire ecosystems adapted slowly to beaver-induced changes [39]. Many animals wreak major changes quickly on the landscape, such as swarming insects or defoliating elephants, but few have had an impact on the scale of beaver technology [40].

Compared to the elaborate engineering projects of beavers, we *Homo sapiens* were very simple builders for most of our evolution. However, as noted earlier, simple toolmaking eventually gave rise to a compounding [8] of tool use, where one tool enabled other tools: a chipped rock made sharp for killing an animal, for example, could also be used to smooth the haft of a spear. Animals use what's at their disposal, and humans were no different. The pace of technology compounded, and while initially glacial, it became exponential: single-edge stone tools maintained the same design from 200,000 to 120,000 BCE [8], but once further adaptations emerged, tool use and development took off—literally—like a rocket!

This ratcheting up of problem-solving capacity and technology is possible because human brains are learning-versatile compared to beaver brains. A major element of human learning before the establishment of cities was that our brains had the capacity, much more so than beavers, to engage in didactic-reproductive learning, generation after generation. At the same time, we also had the capacity, used when the circumstances warranted it, to engage in the development of new knowledge through research-like processes of discovery. When competition came, when the environment changed, when an important prey animal died out or humans moved into different ecosystems, the learning of established ideas through reproductive modes was inadequate by itself. Adaptation was required which, in turn, demanded a different order of learning. Human brains are adaptive and plastic, and adults could shift their thinking somewhat, rewiring neural networks. However, for the young with developing brains who moved with their extended family into new challenges, an upbringing of upheaval geared their brains for discovery mode; they neurologically wired to inquire [41, 42]. A challenge for educators in the twenty-first century, then, is to work out what modes of learning are pertinent in emerging local and global circumstances and what balance can be struck across different modes of teaching and learning, from more didactic to more discovery-oriented. The MELT *facets* and *continuum of learning autonomy* provide the what and how of *Homo sapiens'* transmission-oriented and innovative learning over the course of the last 1000,000 years, as we have always, and need still, to emulate, improvise and innovate.

1.5   One Billion Brains More: The Problems We Face Need Research-Mindedness

Because humans are adept at solving problems, and because our solutions cause more problems, we and the planet are on a destructive trajectory. Education systems that replicate our current successes will also magnify our current problems. Instead, we need educators with broadened perspectives that cope with, and even enjoy, a range of teaching and learning modes. MELT articulate the human capacity to learn didactically and to learn through discovery in ways that reinforce each other. While some educators, parents, researchers and students take a polarised position towards one particular teaching and learning approach, MELT suggest that we need learning environments that explicitly value every point on the learning autonomy continuum This is, arguably, our best hope to move from an inevitable problem-solving/problem-causing loop to a less predetermined future for the Earth.

We need to be able to cover every point on the continuum of teaching and learning approaches, because we need brains that are wired to swing adaptively from learning established knowledge to constructing fresh knowledge. We need brains that are wired to memorise and recall *and* wired to inquire and delve [41]. Education systems need to draw on young children's natural curiosity, promote the acquisition of the massive canon of modern knowledge, *and* be more purposive in how they move between these two.

How can parents, caregivers and early childhood educators help young children's brains to wire in such a way that they love to learn existing knowledge, as well as to discover knowledge on their own? How can these loves be nurtured throughout primary and secondary schooling? What will facilitate the further development of such engaged learning with undergraduates and Master's students, including those who are enrolled in teaching degrees? What difference will this make to Ph.D. students and other researchers when addressing the problems of the Earth? And what will this mean for teachers who engage in their own active and systematic learning, such as action research and ongoing professional development, to improve their students' learning? Further, how can we best nurture a love of moving fluidly across the *continuum of learning autonomy*, rather than prioritising one of the ends?

The above fluidity is one where our genetically-determined neuronal architecture and its adaptive responsiveness to environmental cues [42] forms our brains with not merely the capacity to learn new things, but the capacity to rewire. MELT can inform a rewiring for the next billion brains that is both knowledge-savvy and inquiry-oriented (Fig. 1.5).

Humans have the greatest number of neurons at about seven months' gestation, typically two months before birth [42]. Then apoptosis—healthy, natural cell death—is genetically programmed to remove the less used neurons, so that newborn babies and adults alike have substantially less neurons than we had when we were in the womb [42] where the adult brain has around 80 billion neurons. Typically, those neurons that synapse—or connect—with other neurons survive. These neurons continue the complex process of developing neural networks, with any one neuron connected up to 1,000 other neurons [42] in a mind-boggling array that is the powerhouse of sophisticated thinking.

Most amazing and relevant for MELT is that the number of our synapses—the connections between neurons—goes through the roof early in life, so that by age three we have trillions. But after the age of three, our healthy genetic programming begins to reduce those networks in a process called 'neural pruning' [42]. Our healthy brains go through this natural pruning process where if we don't use it, we lose it: a synapse connection in which two neurons rarely communicate tends to be pruned. The saying is that neurons that fire together wire together [42], meaning that if two

Fig. 1.5 Wired to inquire?

synapsed neurons communicate regularly, they will stay connected and maintain their part of the network. After the age of three, we begin to lose billions of synapses each year, and this process continues through different parts of the brain until the twenties [42]. This sounds bad because learning equates to synapse formation and maintenance. However, neurons and synapses require a lot of energy, and an overly complex network is less efficient and effective.

But here's the thing: what we are sensing, doing, thinking and saying from birth and beforehand (e.g., tasting mother's amniotic fluid as an embryo) influences our synapse formation, and what is pruned [42]. So children who spend the majority of their time using information and communications technology (e.g., gaming) are using their brains in such a way that some neural networks are enhanced and others are limited. As a result, their neuro-architecture—their actual brain's wiring—will reflect their environment [42], just as has always been the case for human brains.

The brain's wiring is a complex mix of genetic determinants and environmental influences. As an extreme example, a baby reared in the dark will not be able to see even when taken into the light at age one [42]. The development of optical pathways in the brain is not only genetically determined but requires environmental stimulus; use it or minimise it.

Learning in the human brain is not compartmentalised into 'cognitive' and 'affective'. Long-term memory is closely associated with the part of the brain called the hippocampus, which itself is also associated with emotions [43]. Correspondingly, a longstanding finding from psychology is that we learn that to which we attend

[44], and so motivational elements are vital for learning [43], frequently in multi-modal ways that reinforce learning [44]. MELT explicitly articulate the cognitive dimensions of engaged learning in concert with the affective dimensions. The beaver in each cartoon at the beginning of each chapter calls out affective-oriented words that connect to the more cognitive facet titles, and this simultaneous connection of cognitive and affective domains is central to MELT, because the connection is true and vital for human learning.

A full range of educational experiences, including face-to-face, hands-on, online and virtual learning, is needed for the education of the next billion brains on the planet. This range of experiences needs to be full not just in terms of subject matter, but in terms of how this subject matter is learned. In MELT terms, this especially concerns the *continuum of learning autonomy*. A full range of educational experiences would embrace teacher-directed immersion of students in content knowledge and in key concepts, as well as student ownership of learning and inclusion in curriculum decisions, where students would be given scope for high levels of autonomy in their learning through investigation, problem-solving and discovery. For the MELT, autonomy ebbs and flows from levels of low *learning autonomy*, with prescribed teaching, through to high levels of *learning autonomy* with teacher boundaries removed, and back again to low *learning aut*onomy. Such shuttling, where students *emulate*, *improvise*, *initiate* and flow back to *emulate* over time, is suggestive of spiralling *learning autonomy* throughout formal education from early childhood through primary and secondary school, to employment, technical study and university, whether a student completes compulsory education, undergraduate study or proceeds to Master's level and Ph.D.

1.6   Structure of This Book

This book's seven-chapter structure mirrors the seven core components of the MELT, the six facets and *learning autonomy*. Each chapter has as its title one of the seven central questions of MELT on a title page comprising a cartoon by Dr. Aaron Humphries [45]. Each cartoon has three characters: a young child, Albert Einstein, and a beaver, each saying something emblematic of the sophisticated thinking pertaining to a particular *facet*. The child sings a line that represents a *facet* from the song *Research Mountain* [21] except in Chap. 7 she says a line from a research article. Einstein says something for each *facet* that connects to sophisticated thinking from the Nobel prize-winning end of the learning spectrum. And the beaver calls out the affective aspect of each *facet*. In each cartoon's banner is the *facet* process, such as *embark and clarify*, and all *facet* processes are double-edged, comprising two strong, interdependent verbs for learning.

This introductory chapter asked, 'What is our purpose?' for student learning, for teaching and for the book itself. This chapter elaborated on the need for, and the possibility of, a coherent solution to the problems associated with an education in which all the parts are not well connected.

Chapter 2 is titled 'What should we use?' and this question is asked in consideration of our educational purposes. Chapter 2 provides a deep sense of the MELT, explaining in detail the six *facets* of sophisticated thinking and a consideration of how much guidance students need in terms of *learning autonomy*. Chapter 2 does this by delving into each facet in turn, interpreted in research stories from primary school (*Place Value* in the Preface), high school (*Parachute* in this chapter, below) and the account of a university graduate (*Silver Fluoride* in Chap. 2). Chapter 2 details the educational literature that informed the creation of MELT, and notes that much of that literature is descriptive in nature and lacks a theoretical underpinning.

Chapter 3 of this book, 'How do we arrange?', provides numerous examples of teachers using MELT to arrange and prompt more sophisticated thinking across the educational trajectory. These examples help to introduce others' pedagogical interpretations of what form MELT had needed to take on and how it needed to be implemented in order for it to work in each of their contexts.

Chapter 4 'What do we trust?' pulls competing theories together in productive tension and places them as the underpinning of MELT. By providing the theoretical underpinning of MELT, the chapter specifically positions competing theories together on the *learning autonomy* continuum, with the aim of arousing awareness and choice of where to operate on or across this continuum.

Chapter 5 is titled 'What does it mean?' and provokes a consideration of seminal and recent learning theories and what they mean for contemporary educational practices and teacher action research in light of MELT. Unpacking and placing learning theories on MELT's *continuum of learning autonomy* is very practical for teacher understanding of theories and for their application of these to classrooms and online learning. Chapter 5 shows the connections between four contemporary learning theories, some of which are perceived to be in direct opposition, and the ways that teacher action research can bring theory to life. The chapter contains a chilling warning of continuing to treat educational theories as competitive rather than complementary, as Machine Teaching comes to the fore.

Chapter 6 asks 'How do we relate?' in regard to humanity's relationship with itself and the planet, and why things seemed to have panned out in a way that leads us inevitably to environmental devastation and social upheaval. The chapter proposes ways in which MELT may be part of a solution that doesn't cause more problems.

Chapter 7, 'How much guidance?' addresses the scaffolding of student learning, using MELT's consideration of learning autonomy. The chapter considers those involved in education and the amount of guidance that may be needed to make MELT work in various settings. Autonomy in MELT is a relationship word, and is intimately connected to 'ownership' of teaching and learning. The need for ownership and empowerment is a major factor when considering how much structure and what sort of guidance is needed by students and teachers alike. The coherence of student learning journeys maybe possible through teachers, parents, schools and universities pulling together in the same direction, as directed by policy, but policy is not so good at motivating that pursuit in the long-term. In order to promote ownership and empowerment, it's good for teachers to be autonomous. But students exposed to a series of overly autonomous teachers may find that their education feels broken and incoherent. How much guidance do we need for teachers and for students?

In summary, this chapter explains the need for the MELT, Chap. 2 details them, and Chap. 3 provides examples from ECE to Ph.D. level. Chapter 4 provides the theoretical underpinning, Chap. 5 considers contemporary learning theories in light of MELT, and Chap. 6 draws together the relationships that MELT may forge. Chapter 7 concludes with considerations for operationalising MELT.

1.7 Conclusion: Student Learning that Resonates

The billion human brains that will be born between 2023 and 2030 need something different from the learning and education that has occurred so far across 100,000 years of human history. That billion will inherit the leadership of the earth somewhere from 2040, with all of the accumulated problems caused by humanity until that time. Those billion need diverse learning environments that resonate with their complex learning capacities, that connect to multiple educator perspectives and theories, and that enable them to address local and global issues in ways that do not cause more problems than they solve. The complexities of human learning demand an expansive and encompassing conceptualisation of learning that mirrors different disciplines, learner ages, teaching theories, learning throughout prehistory and educational research. The billion need to be those whose knowledge, skills, attitudes, values, creativity and discernment are so powerful that they can anticipate problems caused by proposed solutions, and forge solutions that don't cause more problems. The *facets* and their elaboration across the *continuum of learning autonomy* of the MELT are proffered in the next chapter as a conceptualisation that can help address this educational need.

References

1. Einstein Bubble in Cartoon: Isaacson, W. (2007). *Einstein, his life and universe*. London: Simon and Schuster.
2. Dewey, J. (1904/1974). The relation of theory to practice in education. In R. Archambault (Ed.), *John Dewey on Education: Selected Writings* (pp. 315– 338). Chicago: University of Chicago Press.
3. Bundy, A. (Ed.). (2004). *Australian and New Zealand Information Literacy framework: Principles, standards and practice* (5th ed.). Adelaide, Australia: Australian and New Zealand Institute for Information Literacy.
4. Delson, E. (2019, July 10). An early dispersal of modern humans from Africa to Greece. *Nature News and Views*. Retrieved from www.nature.com/articles/d41586-019-02075-9.
5. Stringer, C. (2016). The origin and evolution of Homo sapiens. *Philosophical Transactions of the Royal Society B: Biological Sciences, 371*(1698), 20150237.
6. Tattersall, I. (2016). The thinking primate: Establishing a context for the emergence of modern human cognition. *Proceedings of the American Philosophical Society, 160*(3), 254–265.
7. Scerri, E. M., Thomas, M. G., Manica, A., Gunz, P., Stock, J. T., Stringer, C., et al. (2018). Did our species evolve in subdivided populations across Africa, and why does it matter? *Trends in Ecology & Evolution, 33*(8), 582–594.
8. Koetsier, T. (2019). *The ascent of GIM, the global intelligent machine*. Cham, Switzerland: Springer.

9. van Schaik, C. P., Pradhan, G. R., & Tennie, C. (2019). Teaching and curiosity: Sequential drivers of cumulative cultural evolution in the hominin lineage. *Behavioral Ecology and Sociobiology, 73*(1), 2.

10. Dawkins, R. (1976). *The selfish gene*. Oxford, England: Oxford University Press.

11. Hasan, R. (1995). On social conditions for semiotic mediation: The genesis of mind in society. In A. Sadovnik (Ed.), *Knowledge and pedagogy: The sociology of Basil Bernstein* (pp. 171–196). Norwood, NJ: Ablex.

12. Ritchhart, R., & Perkins, D. (2008). Making thinking visible. *Educational Leadership, 65*(5), 57–61.

13. Wenner, J. A., & Campbell, T. (2017). The theoretical and empirical basis of teacher leadership: A review of the literature. *Review of Educational Research, 87*(1), 134–171.

14. Willison, J. W. (2018). Research skill development spanning higher education: Critiques, curricula and connections. *Journal of University Teaching and Learning Practice, 15*(4), 1.

15. Willison, J., & O'Regan, K. (2007). Commonly known, commonly not known, totally unknown: A framework for students becoming researchers. *Higher Education Research & Development, 26*(4), 393–409.

16. Willison, J. (2012). When Academics integrate research skill development in the curriculum. *Higher Education Research and Development, 31*(6), 905–919.

17. Wilmore, M., & Willison, J. (2016). Graduates' attitudes to research skill development in undergraduate media education. *Asia Pacific Media Educator, 26*(1), 1–16.

18. Bandaranaike, S., & Willison, J. (2015). Building capacity for work-readiness: Bridging the cognitive and affective domains. *Asia-Pacific Journal of Cooperative Education, 16*(3), 223–233.

19. Bandaranaike, S., Snelling, C., Karanicolas, S., & Willison, J. (2012). Opening minds and mouths wider: Developing a model for student reflective practice within clinical placements. In *Proceedings of the 9th International Conference on Cooperative & Work-Integrated Education* (pp. 1–16). Istanbul, Turkey: Bahçeşehir University. Retrieved from https://www.waceinc.org/bahcesehir2012/proceedings.html.

20. Shah, S., Missingham, D., Sabir, F., & Willison, J. (2018). Developing and connecting engineering skills for researching and problem solving. *Journal of University Teaching and Learning Practice, 15*(4), 7.

21. Seebohm, M. (2014). *Research Mountain Song*. Retrieved from https://www.adelaide.edu.au/rsd/schooling/early-childhood/.

22. Lingam, N., Sharma, L., Qaloqiolevu, J., Ramoce, W., Lal, S., & Rafai, R. (2017). i-Talitali framework: Developing a model for engaged learning and teaching in the Pacific. In *Conference Proceedings of the International conference on Models of Engaged Learning and Teaching (I-MELT)*. Adelaide, Australia: Univesity of Adelaide. Retrieved from https://www.adelaide.edu.au/rsd/i-melt/papers/LingamIMELT2017paper.pdf.

23. Monash University (2018). *The Digital Skills Development (DSD) framework*. Retrieved from https://www.monash.edu/__data/assets/pdf_file/0010/1652437/DSD-document.pdf.

24. Willison, J (2019). *The Blended and Engaged Learning Zones (BELZ)*. Retrieved from www.melt.edu.au.

25. Paiva, J., Morais, C., Costa, L., & Pinheiro, A. (2016). The shift from "e-learning" to "learning": Invisible technology and the dropping of the "e". *British Journal of Educational Technology, 47*(2), 226–238.

26. Ain, C. T., Sabir, F., & Willison, J. (2018). Research skills that men and women developed at university and then used in workplaces. *Studies in Higher Education*, 1–13.

27. Willison, J., Sabir, F., & Thomas, J. (2017). Shifting dimensions of autonomy in students' research and employment. *Higher Education Research & Development, 36*(2), 430–443.

28. Willison, J., & Buisman Pijlman, F. (2016). Ph.D. prepared: Research skill development across the undergraduate years. *International Journal of Researcher Development 7*(1), 63–83.

29. Kirschner, P. A., Sweller, J., & Clark, R. E. (2006). Why minimal guidance during instruction does not work: An analysis of the failure of constructivist, discovery, problem-based, experiential, and inquiry-based teaching. *Educational Psychologist, 41*(2), 75–86.

30. Hmelo-Silver, C. E., Duncan, R. G., & Chinn, C. A. (2007). Scaffolding and achievement in problem-based and inquiry learning: A response to Kirschner, Sweller, and Clark. *Educational Psychologist, 42*(2), 99–107.
31. Gray, R. D., Drummond, A. J., & Greenhill, S. J. (2009). Language phylogenies reveal expansion pulses and pauses in Pacific settlement. *Science, 323*(5913), 479–483.
32. Willison, J. W. (2000). *Classroom factors affecting student scientific literacy: Tales and their interpretation using a metaphoric framework* (Unpublished doctoral dissertation, Curtin University, Perth, Australia). Retrieved from https://espace.curtin.edu.au/handle/20.500. 11937/268.
33. Neubauer, S., Hublin, J. J., & Gunz, P. (2018). The evolution of modern human brain shape. *Science Advances, 4*(1), eaao5961.
34. Martin, L. D., & Bennett, D. K. (1977). The burrows of the Miocene beaver Palaeocastor, western Nebraska, USA. *Palaeogeography, Palaeoclimatology, Palaeoecology, 22*(3), 173–193.
35. Kornienko, T. V. (2009). Notes on the cult buildings of northern Mesopotamia in the Aceramic Neolithic period. *Journal of Near Eastern Studies, 68*(2), 81–102.
36. Odling-Smee, F. J. (1995). Niche construction, genetic evolution and cultural change. *Behavioural Processes, 35*(1–3), 195–205.
37. Patenaude, F. (1984). The ontogeny of behavior of free-living beavers (Castor canadensis). *Zeitschrift für Tierpsychologie, 66*(1), 33–44.
38. Latham, N. R., & Mason, G. J. (2008). Maternal deprivation and the development of stereotypic behaviour. *Applied Animal Behaviour Science, 110*(1–2), 84–108.
39. Jones, C. G., Lawton, J. H., & Shachak, M. (1994). Organisms as ecosystem engineers. In *Ecosystem management* (pp. 130–147). New York, NY: Springer.
40. Hugueney, M., & Escuillie, F. (1996). Fossil evidence for the origin of behavioral strategies in early Miocene Castoridae, and their role in the evolution of the family. *Paleobiology, 22*(4), 507–513.
41. Willison, J. (2013). Inquiring ape? *Higher Education Research and Development, 32*(5), 861–865.
42. Styles, J. (2008). *The fundamentals of brain development: Integrating nature & nurture.* Cambridge, MA: Harvard University Press.
43. Tambini, A., Rimmele, U., Phelps, E. A., & Davachi, L. (2017). Emotional brain states carry over and enhance future memory formation. *Nature Neuroscience, 20*(2), 271.
44. Leong, Y. C., Radulescu, A., Daniel, R., DeWoskin, V., & Niv, Y. (2017). Dynamic interaction between reinforcement learning and attention in multidimensional environments. *Neuron, 93*(2), 451–463.
45. Humphrey, A. (2014). Beyond graphic novels: Illustrated scholarly discourse and the history of educational comics. *Media International Australia, 151*(1), 73–80.

Chapter 2

What will we use?

Find & Generate

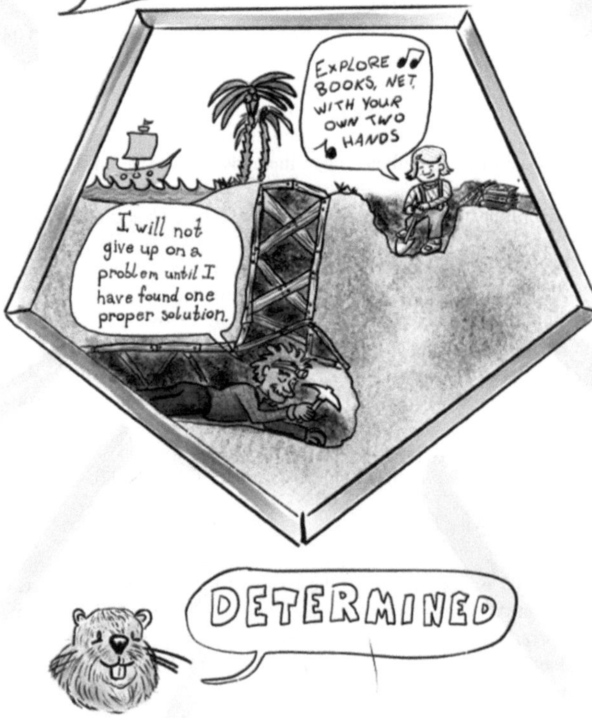

Chapter 2
What Will We Use?

2.1 Introducing the Models of Engaged Learning and Teaching

This chapter provides a deep and nuanced understanding of the Models of Engaged Learning and Teaching. Together, these models comprise much of what we may use across education to connect human brain development and education theory to diverse practice. Each of the models shares the six *facets* of sophisticated thinking that were foreshadowed in Chap. 1 through the analysis of *Parachute,* as well as the consideration of *learning autonomy* that is detailed below. The focus of Chap. 1 was on the role of education as a means of developing learners born from 2023 to 2030, who will be the problem-solvers, critical thinkers and researchers leading the planet from 2040. In order to achieve that purpose, the logic of Chap. 1 naturally led to the need for a conceptual framework that is broadly representative, across many perspectives, of learning and ideas about learning and teaching. Thus, Chapter 2 addresses this identified need by presenting the MELT as a viable option for a conceptualisation that we can use to span education and connect disparate parts.

In Sect. 2.2, this chapter presents an account from a university graduate who developed MELT skills at university and used these after graduation. Then Sects. 2.3.1–2.3.6 detail the six *facets* of MELT, including their affective domain, guiding questions and descriptions, and *learning autonomy*. Section 2.3.7 considers sophisticated learning as spiralling, recursive and messy and looks at the ethical and social dimensions of MELT. Section 2.4 in conclusion, is about engagement, adaptability, fluidity and ownership.

© The Author(s) 2020
J. Willison, *The Models of Engaged Learning and Teaching,*
SpringerBriefs in Education, https://doi.org/10.1007/978-981-15-2683-1_2

2.1.1 A Holistic View

The MELT don't provide grounds for a proposal that education should develop
new theorisations or characteristics. Rather, the aim is to consolidate the past
100 years of research and reflect human learning over the past 100,000 years in
the MELT. Taken individually, each MELT *facet* and the consideration of *learning autonomy* is, in many respects, common, unsurprising and even too familiar. To
reduce the effect of 'familiarity breeding contempt', the facets and learning autonomy are presented in a way that is intended to bring them to life, re-kindling a
sense of their importance and demonstrating their synergistic power when taken as
a whole. In order to achieve this, each *facet* and *learning autonomy* level is considered through the perspective of three educational contexts: primary schooling
(*Place Value* from the preface), middle years of schooling (*Parachute* from Chap. 1)
and a volunteering situation of a university graduate (*Silver Fluoride*, below).
Through these multiple perspectives, the richness and complexity of each MELT
facet and *learning autonomy* are partially revealed.

However, it is only possible to fully understand the MELT by perceiving the
resonant energy of the set of *facets* and the continuum of *learning autonomy* together.
This potential, this energy is more complex to convey. The stories give some idea
of how the *facets* and *learning aut*onomy work together, functioning as indivisible
parts of one precious jewel. Just as no facet of a jewel exists in isolation, all the *facets*
of MELT work together to crystallise into something of shape and enduring beauty.

While the set of *facets* must be understood holistically, it can be helpful to delineate
sophisticated thinking into separate facets. MELT takes what often remains implicit in
education—the skills of sophisticated thinking—and makes them explicit. *Learning
autonomy* intersects with the six *facets* of MELT in unpredictable, nonlinear ways.
As noted in Chap. 1, the facets of MELT represent the 'what' of learning, while
the *continuum of learner autonomy* represents the 'how', that is, the way in which
the facets are operationalised by teachers and brought to life for students. In MELT,
learning autonomy is considered to be a 'relationship' word, connecting learners to
each other, to teachers and to the learning context.

This chapter pays more attention to the facet *embark & clarify* than to the other
facets. This is because it is difficult to convey the sense of purpose epitomised by
embark & clarify; students often find it hard to work out what their teachers want
them to do, or work out what they themselves will pursue. This difficulty is partly
down to the fact that there are so many different ways to *embark & clarify* and the
subject and discipline differences of how to begin often eclipse the similarities of
complex starting processes. When learning something new, it is essential to begin
correctly and to become increasingly clear about one's direction; the other five facets
of the MELT depend absolutely on getting the purpose right. Except in the case of
the simplest forms of learning, the embarking processes require clarification, often
many times, over extended periods. It can be necessary to re-embark on a project
time and again and re-clarify direction and purpose. The stories *Place Value* and
Parachute, from primary schooling and secondary schooling, respectively, and the

Silver Fluoride account (from a university graduate, below) provide an understanding of the richness of the facet and the challenges it poses for engaged learning and teaching. A clear sense of how to *embark & clarify* frequently emerges out of the other five facets, with the end of one journey becoming the beginning of the next. A description of the familiar aspects that comprise the MELT follows.

2.1.2 The Origins of the MELT

The MELT began with a blank whiteboard and a question: what are we as teachers doing when we facilitate sophisticated student thinking? The resources that Kerry O'Regan and I used to answer this question were the literature and reflections on our teaching of well-scaffolded inquiry-based learning [2]. The *facets* of the MELT's were informed by the Australian and New Zealand Institute of Information Literacy (ANZIIL) standards [3], the Structure of Observed Learning Outcomes (SOLO) taxonomy [4] and Bloom's taxonomies [5, 6]. Bloom's taxonomies consist of two separate hierarchical frameworks with fundamentally different premises for the cognitive domain [5] and the affective domain [6]. The values, attitudes and emotions associated with the affective domain are embedded in each MELT *facet*. This means that the MELT comprise one framework with cognitive domain and affective domain integrated into the *facets*.

A crucial intentional structural feature of MELT is that it represents the affective domain but does not elaborate on it. Affective aspects are presented using single-word adjectives describing a learner, whereas cognitive aspects are described and elaborated much more richly. This is not because the cognitive aspects are more important than the affective aspects. Rather, it is because assessing affect is risky [7]: assessing something so important yet difficult to probe can be counterproductive. However, the affective aspects are pivotal for whether learning happens or not. For example, students are more likely to learn if they are willing to take risks, where, for example, a creative writing student who's encouraged to experiment is more likely to come up with an original metaphor.

The design intention for MELT was to enable a conceptualisation that ran from primary school to post-graduation [8]. Most educational continua represent an increase from lower ability to higher, from less sophisticated to more sophisticated thinking. Yet each student potentially engages in thinking that is sophisticated within the context of their current educational level. Rather than describing an incremental, linear type of improvement, Kerry and I perceived a need to describe a continuum that spiralled so that it could represent learning from ECE to Ph.D. level, flowing throughout the years of education. This is because any domain with a linear increase will struggle to remain pertinent across the whole educational trajectory, and is therefore not helpful for forging connections across education.

2.1.3 Learning Autonomy

The *continuum of learning autonomy* [8] in the MELT is a way of describing an educative scaffolding process that may spiral over terms, semesters and years of education and is identical in character to, and informed by, Vygotsky's zone of proximal development [9]. As noted in Chap. 1, for the MELT, learning autonomy involves the movement of students between lower and higher levels of control over their own learning; back and forth, like the tides [10]. Table 2.1 shows more detail than Chap. 1 for a version of MELT that is designed for teachers, where educator scope for autonomy is delineated into five levels.

Learning autonomy emerged in our early research as a decisive factor for helping educators to conceive of ways to facilitate the learning of the *facets*, and to understand the ways in which students were actually performing [8, 11]. Drawing on Dewey [12] and the science education literature, we used terminology like 'closed inquiry and 'open inquiry' [13] for the endpoints of the continuum. 'Scaffolded' was a mid-point between 'closed' and 'open', and this three-level framing still seemed to leave educational leaps in the continuum that were conceptually too far in practice for students. So two levels on either side of 'scaffolded' were added, giving five levels.

A student-oriented three-level version of *learning autonomy* and teacher 'proximity' was developed, comprising emulate, improvise and initiate as mentioned in Chap. 1, and shown in more detail in Table 2.2. Three levels are in keeping with levels of delineation that have been widely used to convey Vygotsky's ZPD from a teacher's perspective; model, scaffold and fade [14].

There is no clear border between the end of one level and the beginning of another. Interpretation of autonomy is dependent on a deep knowledge of context and students, and the *continuum of learning autonomy* is a tool for planning and analysing, not for measuring in ways that produce meaningful numbers (though we tried this approach initially) [15]. The overlap between educator-provided scope for *learning* autonomy and student *learning* autonomy as experienced by them is shown in Table 2.3.

Table 2.1 Teacher extent of scope for *learning autonomy*

Prescribed	Bounded	Scaffolded	Open-ended	Unbounded
Highly structured directions and modelling from educator prompt learning, in which…	Boundaries set and limited directions from educator channel learning in which…	Scaffolds placed by educator shape independent learning, in which…	Students initiate, with guidance from the educator.	Students determine guidelines for learning that are in accord with subject, discipline or context.

Table 2.2 Three-level continuum of learner autonomy

Emulate	Improvise	Initiate
Follow your teacher's lead, so that you learn ways of doing things and about things.	Work creatively within your teacher's guidelines and *improve* or adapt what was given to you.	You drive the learning, deciding your purpose and how to achieve it.

Table 2.3 Overlap between teacher scope for learning autonomy and the continuum of learning autonomy

Scope for Learning Autonomy (provided by educators)				
Prescribed	Bounded	Scaffolded	Open-ended	Unbounded
Emulate		Improvise		Initiate

Continuum of Learning Autonomy (what students do)

For each facet, consideration can be made for the level of educator-planned learner autonomy, called the *scope for learning autonomy*, and the actual autonomy that students work with, called simply *learning autonomy*, shown together in Table 2.3. This delineation between teacher intention (scope) and actual student learning autonomy is important for three reasons:

1. It clarifies the difference between teaching intentions and the lived reality of students.
2. It provides insights into the process of differentiating the curriculum, so that each student is more able to engage in the learning that they are ready for.
3. It challenges our concepts of assessment, including what is assessed and why. This is because many assessments place a uniform demand on student *learning autonomy*, as a result of which some students are under-prepared and others are under-challenged.

MELT are able to connect ECE to Ph.D., across disciplinary and transdisciplinary contexts, because the *learning autonomy* question is always pertinent across formal education: 'how much structure and guidance do students need?

2.2 Silver Fluoride

The higher education perspective given below in *Silver Fluoride* is an account by Kevin, a graduate whose oral health degree was influenced by MELT. In an interview, Kevin reflects on his planning for a volunteer placement in rural Cambodia after graduation, and what happened when he went and enacted his plans with the people in that country. The version of MELT that Kevin's degree used was the Research Skill Development (RSD) framework, and this influenced the terminology that Kevin uses to describe his sophisticated thinking. Kevin's account and the earlier stories *Place Value* and *Parachute* are then used together to bring the seven core characteristics of MELT to life across the years of learning.

Silver Fluoride

Before I left for Cambodia yes—because I actually took a silver fluoride which is a product that we didn't even actually come into contact with in the Bachelor of Oral Health here. When we went for a placement for Canberra there was a tutor there that was working with us and she used it [silver fluoride] because she trained I think in Darwin or somewhere out and she was working out in the sticks and so they had that as a prevention for decay and all that sort of stuff so they were using that product a lot, but we didn't come into contact with it because it stains teeth and there's all these things that they don't like aesthetically so that's why we weren't using it, but it's like an amazing product because I was really looking into that because I thought that might be really beneficial for Cambodia because they don't get care often and they're considered more rural so I was doing a lot of research with that and I ended up purchasing some and taking it over with me and I was using it when I was over there [16].

2.3   Student Experiences of MELT Facets and Autonomy

The stories *Place Value* and *Parachute,* along with Kevin's account in *Silver Fluoride*, are used next to provide a deep understanding of each of the MELT facet's verb couplets, affective adjective, key question, detail and then a consideration of the *extent of learning autonomy* for that *facet*.

2.3.1   *Embark & Clarify*

Process	Affective dimension	Question
Embark & clarify	Curious	What is our purpose?

Detail: Students respond to, or initiate their own, direction, and clarify it while considering ethical, cultural, social and team (ECST) issues.

To *embark* is to begin the journey, but how do students *clarify* what their purpose actually is? Do they know their starting point, where they are going and how they might get there? There are many different ways of commencing. This variety of starting points is not only due to the fact that different disciplines have different processes and terminologies, but also because sophisticated thinking is non-linear; it jumps around and is hard to capture. Embarking processes often require other *facets* of MELT to be actuated before what is embarked on becomes fully clarified. For example, in disciplines that start with a research question, where did that research question come from? Who framed it, and how did that educator, student or team come to that phrasing? Formal research questions sometimes start as questions of speculation and wondering about possibilities, or some intellectual dissonance that makes one curious. Sometimes the questions emerge as a synthesis of the literature, through conversations, or by clarification through teaching, and these typically require all the facets of the MELT.

The intentionally general verb *embark* is the first facet listed here because it is a logical starting point. However, it is frequently not the first facet that students begin within their learning endeavours. Sometimes we stumble on an issue or idea, sometimes we are inspired by curiosity about a phenomenon or issue, and sometimes we immerse ourselves in a lot of reading around a topic. Formal research questions are typically a 're-embarking'. That is, they follow on from a research journey that has involved much reading and synthesising of literature, observation, piloting, hypothesising, discussing, reflecting and deciding about which of all possible questions is the best one to pursue. The same is true for the processes of defining problems when problem-solving, or clarifying what decisions need to be made in evidence-based decision-making: the process of formulating a point of embarkation and clarifying takes time. The point of departure is so complex that it commonly requires all six facets of MELT to clarify and re-embark.

For students, a sense of purpose is vital in the voyage of discovery that we call learning. However, a sense of purpose is difficult to nurture if learning is prescribed by teachers, because compulsion or coercion increases the risk of compliance, where the purpose is stated and injected rather than internalised by the learner themselves. On the other hand, when students choose the direction of their own learning, there are many complexities for them and their teachers to deal with if they are to become clear about their purpose.

The central question for *embark & clarify* is 'What is our purpose?' The verbs *embark & clarify* and the question are in the plural form because of the social dynamic in teaching and learning. However, 'What is my purpose?' is the question for a student to ask themselves if engaged in an individual project. For educators trying to launch students into sophisticated (but guided) learning, the question is 'How do I convey the purpose to students?' Like all other facets, the nature of this facet can sometimes be better understood through the key question. Even better, the combination of the process verbs, description, key question and affective domain descriptor together provide a well-rounded sense of the parameters of a particular facet. To understand the mentality behind MELT, it is essential to understand the characteristics of each facet, for each MELT facet must be set into its context, and adaptations are typically required. Nowhere is the need for adaptation truer than the word of *embark*, which is almost always too general to be of direct use with students.

Embark emerged from the first ANZIIL standard, 'Recognises the need for knowledge' [3], which is one of the dozens of ways of commencing complex thinking. 'Embark' includes asking, hypothesising, identifying problems or patient needs, aims, goals or potential, immersion in a reading, story or context, and so on. It is an intentionally general verb, and its conceptual power lies in its inclusion of multiple ways of beginning. In particular, it embraces the numerous ways in which sophisticated thinking begins, as operationalised by those who know best; the teachers, academics, tutors, parents and students. *Embark* connotes a journey, a voyage of discovery where there may be many points of disembarking and re-embarking, as well as hidden or anticipated perils. *Clarify* suggests an ongoing process, where things may be initially muddy, which is OK as long as clarity comes over time: 'In a world deluged by irrelevant information, clarity is power' [17].

The facet *embark & clarify* also addresses one of the holes in Bloom's taxonomy: because Bloom's research strategy was to gather teachers' perspectives, the hierarchy has content knowledge as the foundational taxon, and so is suggestive of learning always commencing with content knowledge. This is frequently the case in education, but by no means is it or should it be always the case. As a hierarchical structure, Bloom's taxonomy locked in a mentality of content knowledge acquisition first, whereas MELT treats Bloom's verbs as fluid, non-sequential, but vital. Knowledge is always important in learning, but it is not always the starting point, especially in the context of connected learning that happens online.

The ethical, social and cultural considerations of engaged learning are the only elements mentioned in two facets, in *embark & clarify* and in *communicate & apply*. The six ANZIIL Standards, as the starting point for the six facets, articulated the ethical, social and cultural dimensions in the 'standard' concerned with communication. However, in 2012, a review of the facets by a variety of academics who had used MELT led to their strong demand that ethical, social and cultural dimensions also be represented not only in *communicate & apply*, but also *embark & clarify*. The academics perceived that the ethical, social and cultural dimensions were so crucial to engaged learning that they needed to be explicit first and last. The reasons for this come through clearly in *Silver Fluoride*, as Kevin engages with people living in villages in Cambodia through the use of an outmoded Oral Health treatment. Kevin's ethical decision is to prioritise dental health over aesthetics in that context, rightly or wrongly. There is always the need for teachers to consider the ethical, social and cultural dimensions first and last, and for students to learn to do so.

In terms of the social dimension, often people embark on sophisticated learning individually. However, MELT articulations tend to be in a plural form, for example, 'embark' rather than 'embarks', to emphasise the social aspects of learning. Education frequently entails social interaction, with the teacher and other students playing a major role in the learning environment even when students are working individually, as shown in *Parachute*. Determining purpose as an individual is difficult, and it is often even more complicated for teams to mutually develop a sense of direction that is clear to all involved.

The ethical and cultural elements of sophisticated thinking often do or should dictate direction, and need to be considered early in order to avoid conflict and unfair or adversarial processes or outcomes. The sorts of questions teachers or students ask, project goals they set or problems they identify all are best scrutinised from an ethical perspective, early on. For example, a project in mathematics that asks 'What did the ancient Greeks contribute to trigonometry?' may steer students away from all the work that happened in the Middle East between the era of the last influential Greek mathematicians (around 2,200 years ago) [18] and the mathematical concepts' reception in Europe (about 900 years ago) [19]. The 1,300 years in between saw much translation, development and addition of concepts by scholars in the Middle East and India, so they ended up not just with the Greeks' trigonometry, but also the Arabic–Hindu number system (that is the same system used currently in the West, including in *Place Value*), algebra and sophisticated trigonometry applications, all from the Middle East and India [19]. A culturally aware question, instead of the one above, would be "Who contributed to the development of trigonometry, and what were their contributions?" This leaves the question open, rather than eliminating entire cultures' contributions. Of course, the process could be scaffolded: "What did the ancient Greeks contribute to Trigonometry" could be asked first, then 'What did the Middle East contribute to Trigonometry?" Alternatively, different cultures could be allocated to teams who would be asked to report back to the whole class.

This example necessarily throws up ethical dimensions too: is it ethical to give no attribution of ideas to their developers? The wrong or incomplete attribution of ideas could be seen as unethical, a form of plagiarism. Therefore, it makes sense that ethical and cultural dimensions are located also in *communicate & apply*, where, for example, citation issues may be portrayed as ethical and cultural issues, rather than as a bureaucratic enterprise. So the ethical, cultural and social dimensions need to be part of the product or outcomes of sophisticated thinking, but especially integral to the learning processes of *communicating & applying* and *embarking & clarifying*.

In *Parachute*, Shelly decided to explore differences in parachute shapes, while Katie emulated the teacher's lead to explore differences in materials. Shelly in effect self-identified 'shape' as her independent variable, and to do so required high levels of cognitive ability. She also operationalised this independent variable using two shapes: square versus round parachute. Katie, following a process that had been modelled by the teacher, faced the difficult prospect of clarifying and understanding the teacher's intention in order to answer the question, 'what is my purpose?' Shelly embarked by posing a research question, and then she seemed to formulate a null hypothesis 'If the key factors are the same, the parachute should come down at the same rate'. However, in the simple structures of Year 8 science, students were asked merely for an aim. Whether embarkation entails developing an aim, a research question, a hypothesis, a null hypothesis or a combination of these, serious work is typically required to conceptualise and articulate a way of embarking.

For Kevin in *Silver Fluoride*, embarking involved clarifying the aims of his visit to Cambodia around the general idea of providing dental help to people who usually received none, all on a volunteer's budget. Embarking for him involved the process of getting to the question 'what would happen if I used silver fluoride?' This question was prompted by his memory of a placement experience from his degree where a tutor had mentioned silver fluoride use with people in remote contexts. As his bachelor's degree did not cover silver fluoride formally, Kevin needed to be open-minded in order to consider whether this compound could be relevant in the context of a developing nation. The ethical and social issues were paramount, as dentists in developed nations have stopped using silver fluoride due to cosmetic concerns [20]. But Kevin inferred that rural Cambodians would prioritise keeping their teeth over concerns about stained teeth. Kevin could have been wrong, and this was an ethically, culturally and socially charged endeavour in which he took a calculated risk.

The children in *Place Value* were in play mode around the tree, and were driven by curiosity and mimicry of other children, engaging with the familiar and the unfamiliar. The children were having fun doing what they wanted; the curriculum was unknown to me as an observer, but the learning seemed to be substantial. The children were also driven by an impetus towards togetherness, and this togetherness did not restrict their individual exploration.

Some of those children were in the classroom the next day, and had to understand the complex ideas underlying the mathematical concept of 'place value'. However, it was difficult for them to read the term correctly, let alone anticipate or deduce the purpose of the activity. Nevertheless, the children were lively and enjoyed raising their voices in a chant with the teacher. It is not clear whether students were able to connect the original chant of 'place value' to the sequencing activity they engaged in. But we will see in later facets how complex the 'place value' concept is, and how the concept itself is a voyage of discovery requiring many points of embarking and re-embarking before it can be fully grasped.

Embark & clarify, the MELT verb-pair denoting commencement, has proven to be fit-for-purpose because it is necessarily broad. As such, it encapsulates the many starting and re-starting points required for engaged learning and teaching, from clarifying what a teacher wants, to determining what a patient needs, to selecting independent variables, to wondering what to play with under a tree. You will see in Chap. 3 that there are many ways educators and students have brought *embark & clarify* to life, and that teachers choose verbs that are appropriate, context-based ways of commencing. Example verbs that educators have used for 'embark' include the following:

- Ask,
- Question,
- Specify aim,
- Determine goal,
- Define problem,
- Define specifications,
- Diagnose need,
- Identify issue,
- Recognise,
- Speculate,
- Immerse,
- Probe.

Affective aspects

Embarking is complex and, like all the facets, involves an interaction between the cognitive and the affective. Shelly's willingness to break away from the teacher's example was full of risks. Was she driven by some curiosity—provoked by an interest in shapes or a TV show on parachute design? Was she driven by the prospect of getting higher marks because she did not merely follow the teacher's example? Whatever drove her prompted a resilience, because throughout the difficult process, she kept going.

It is possible that the children playing in *Place Value* barely noticed their learning, and it's not likely that they consciously worked out what they were going to play. Rather, their decision-making was intuitive, spontaneous and curiosity driven. Open-slather learning can be bewildering, but somehow young children find it in themselves to play and learn in very unpredictable ways. In contrast, the children over seven playing nearby chose a fun activity (volleyball) with known and challenging parameters. There is a big difference between autonomous play and playing a game with pre-set rules. In terms of measured outcomes, students may learn more as a result of direct instruction than play, but that doesn't mean that the learning which comes from direct instruction is deeper, more comprehensive or more useful. It may merely be more measurable. While the ability of students to propose researchable questions is legitimately assessable, affective aspects of *embark & clarify*, like 'curiosity', are much more difficult to measure. This doesn't make curiosity less valuable or important; rather, it means that the complex and vital affective domain needs to be thoughtfully taken into consideration by educators in all learning design.

In *Place Value*, the maths learning was at the opposite end of the autonomy spectrum to the play around the tree, with a specified curriculum and predetermined answers. However, the teacher rarely corrected any child, instead gave cues like pauses in pointing at numbers, and silences. Then she continued, asking, 'is any number in the wrong place?' and gave students time to ponder. Perhaps most important, she structured in opportunities for student self-correction later in the sequence of events. She operated with tact, sensing that students needed feedback, but that feedback needed to be sensitive and non-accusatory in nature and, as much as possible, to come from other students. Terms like 'maths anxiety' spring to mind, especially if a child is struggling with more basic aspects of the lesson, like reading a number as 'fourteen' instead of 'forty-one'. For the teacher, the affective dimension of that lesson may have been something akin to 'soothing' or 'reconciling', rather than curiosity.

In terms of ethical, social and cultural aspects, the teacher used the powerful influence of spatial togetherness on the *italitali* mat and chanting of terminology to weave a sense of social cohesion and support. For students, to even pronounce the term 'place value' was challenging; initially, the students seemed to be confounded by another maths term, reading the flashcard as 'plus value'. Some of their earlier experiences with pairs of numbers placed side by side would doubtless have involved addition, which may have led to their confusion. So the knowledge base they needed to draw on was shifting, becoming more sophisticated and more abstract. The concept of 'place value' changes everything, and the students needed to work out what this teacher wanted them to do with this place that was supposed to be so valuable, but which maybe didn't seem as valuable as their tree place by the water. The question of what students 'value' influences every face-to-face class interaction, including for students who prefer and value online worlds.

The affective descriptor for *embark & clarify* needs to be responsive to context. For Kevin to begin to probe the merits of a medication which was not authorised in his degree, he was driven by empathy for the people of rural Cambodia. Kevin and eight other university students who completed the Bachelor of Oral Health were interviewed one year after completion. Analysis of the interviews showed that for them, *embark & clarify* was complex in the affective domain, initiated by numerous and diverse interactions, and seemed to be much more nuanced and context-sensitive than any other facet [21]. Sometimes, sophisticated thinking is driven by curiosity, sometimes by empathy for patient needs and sometimes by passion for an issue [16]. This starting point may be initiated by a teacher, as shown in the class context of *Place Value*, and in such cases, the challenge is to clarify what the teacher wants. In cases where the starting point is initiated by a student, the process of clarification can end up being even more complex, with students needing to fine-tune the question, aim or need. In addition to *curious*, the study in the Oral Health context found other affective descriptors that impelled graduates to *embark*: passion, ownership, interest in learning, implications of not researching, boredom and the need to justify [16]. Therefore research is showing that *embarking & clarifying* has, to date, the most complex cognitive and affective domains. An implication is that this facet requires more context-specific modelling by teachers than currently occurs, more practice in diverse contexts and more explicit connections between contexts. If that all were to occur, then the metacognition of students in relation to how they *embark* will be enhanced, and they will develop a sense of purpose for their own learning.

Einstein looked to the affective domain to explain his success as a learner: 'I am not especially gifted or talented. I am only very, very curious' [22]. Einstein's self-characterisation is one reason that 'curious' is used as a placeholder for affect in MELT. However, other affective descriptors are often more pertinent to the context and should be chosen carefully by educators or students and used instead. At times, identifying excess and deficit affect associated with each facet is useful, and for *embark & clarify* these are *obsessive* and *disengaged,* respectively.

Autonomy

Each facet may place its own demands on students, experience by learning experience, task by task, assessment by assessment, project by project, including how much autonomy is provided and how much each student operates with. The two stories and the graduate account are next compared and contrasted in terms of *learner autonomy* in order to elucidate this concept. The children playing under the tree embarked with a high level of autonomy, with no obvious supervision. They determined what they would play, where, with whom and for how long. But the next day in the maths class, three of those same children were grappling with the teacher's aim for the lesson. Their embarkation was highly prescribed and required sophisticated and abstract thinking. The students had an oral familiarity with numbers, but found it difficult to get the right-to-left orientation correct. It was daunting for them to understand what value a specific place or location gave a numeral compared to another numeral. The class embarked on learning content knowledge specified by the teacher and with which few students were familiar, and this required much clarification and re-clarification.

Kevin determined to explore the value of silver fluoride without boundaries set by others. The potential risks and benefits of the substance were his to weigh up, and his *innovative* approach may have led to some severe problems. His decision to act in such an autonomous way may have been driven by his empathy for the people, his curiosity about a now-abandoned medical approach, or any number of other affective factors.

Shelly took the opportunity to pose her own question, about parachute shape, *improvising* in a way that was in keeping with the *scaffolded* scope provided, with some teacher parameters and occasional guidance. Katie, in the same classroom, *emulated* the teacher's example and stuck to a prescribed question about parachute material.

Shelly's method of embarkation resulted in different ramifications to Katie's. Shelly's own choice of independent variable led to unanticipated problems, making engagement with the other MELT facets substantially more complex than it was for Katie. The surprising element in *Parachute* is that Shelly seemed so clear so quickly about her direction, and never wavered from it. Even though she experienced multiple problems and hold-ups as she *improvised* and *innovated*, she actually submitted her final report on time, along with others who *emulated* the teacher's modelling. For many students, regardless of educational level, this quick clarification would not have happened, and they would consequently have failed to submit a report of any substance. The pressures are often against a student to be too innovative, and sometimes the perceived or actual risk causes students to emulate instead.

The two school stories and the graduate's account show the diverse range of student autonomy that was evident for *embark & clarify*. A similarly diverse range of autonomy was also evident in the case of the other facets, as shown below. Table 2.4 summarises the highest level of autonomy that was observed for each facet as demonstrated by participants in the stories and account.

Table 2.4 The highest level of *learning autonomy* evident for each facet, story by story

Facet	Place Value		Parachute		Silver Fluoride
	Children around tree	Children in class	Shelly	Katie	Kevin
Embark & clarify	Initiate	Emulate	Improvises	Emulates	Initiates
Find & generate	Initiate	Emulate	Improvises	Emulates	Initiates
Evaluate & reflect	Initiate	Emulate	Initiates	Emulates	Initiates
Organise & manage	Initiate	Emulate	Initiates	Emulates	Initiates
Analyse & synthesise	Initiate	Improvise	Initiates	Emulates	Initiates
Communicate & apply	Initiate	Improvise	Improvises	Emulates	Initiates

Within the same learning context, different students work at differing points on the *continuum of learning autonomy*, regardless of teacher intention, and this is seen in *Parachute*. Some students frequently seek out clarification, ask what is next, request specified processes, and pursue a multitude of ways of working with the autonomy akin to *emulate*, regardless of whether the teacher provides a learning task that is engineered for students to *improvise* or *initiate*. In *Parachute*, Katie emulated the teacher's model for all six facets, while Shelly initiated *evaluating, organising* and *analysing* and improvised in the other three *facets*. Same classroom facilitation, with two very different student experiences. The same six-year-olds in *Place Value* were playing highly autonomously one day and learning with *prescribed* facilitation the next. This demonstrates that, in MELT, autonomy is not a characteristic that one acquires, but something which varies according to the relationship of a learner to teachers, other learners and the context.

2.3.2 Find & Generate

Process	Affective dimension	Question
Find & generate	Determined	What will we use?

Detail: Students *find* information and tools, and generate data/ideas using appropriate methodologies.

The MELT facet *find & generate* is concerned with using methods to make available elements that we will use, as dictated by a particular purpose. These 'elements' could be the information or data needed to address a research question—tables of results from published articles, for example, or data from one's own experiments. Elements could be physical or electronic tools, equipment or manuscripts. A chemist once said 'A couple of months in the chemistry lab can save you a couple of hours in the library' [23]. This facetious comment, written before the advent of the Internet, is a reminder that seeking already-existing information can prevent the unnecessary wastage of resources required to generate data. Seeking others' information or generating one's own data both require methodologies that are learned over time and that are context-specific.

Kevin the graduate was prompted by his impending visit to consider whether silver fluoride may be useful in Cambodian villages. With this purpose in mind, his self-determined need was to look up product and usage information, find out about side effects, and consider the costs, packing and customs requirements associated with taking silver fluoride overseas. When in Cambodia, he also had to *find* patients whose needs were well-suited to his treatment and not apply a one-size-fits-all strategy. Shelly's task looks more complex, as she needed to generate primary data and a protocol to achieve this, as well as coming to the realisation that she had to control the size of the parachute, and therefore use mathematical equations to calculate its optimal area.

The six-year-olds in *Place Value* had to *find* the 'place' that bestows value on numerals. For each two-digit number, the six-year-olds had to locate the numeral on the left and interpret it differently than if it was by itself. This was not at all straight-forward, as evidenced when the students read 'forty-one' as 'fourteen', and the group of eight students inserted forty-one immediately after eleven in the sequence of numbers. Finding the right 'place' made all the difference in terms of determining the correct number sequence, and the task was initially beyond the understanding of almost the whole class. We wouldn't normally think of reading two-digit numbers as 'finding', but that may be because we forget how difficult the task is the first time around, when reading numbers of more than one digit requires locating the left-hand numeral in a two-digit number and assigning that number a special value. Locating the place of value was potentially bewildering for those who did not know their left hand from their right.

When three of the six-year-olds were playing around the tree the day before the maths lesson, they had many shells, seeds and other objects to *find*. Sometimes, the objects which they found prompted what they would do—a natural 'object-based' learning [24]. This type of learning was less about working out someone else's (cryptic) meaning about, for example, where 'place value is found'. The type of learning was more about a way of finding that gave way to more finding, as when a child found a specific shell and suddenly noticed specimens of the same shell all around them. The potential for finding was rich, with new things constantly being washed up, blown in or dropped down. As the seasons changed, so did the weather, the texture of the bark, and the character of nearby flowers and seeds. What was findable in and under the tree provided a rich learning environment that prompted the children to engage in multifaceted sophisticated thinking.

Affect

The place-holding affective adjective for *find & generate* is *determined*—a deter-mined student pushing on to *find* relevant and useful information or to generate data. Shelly epitomises this, as even in an eighty-minute episode she was fierce in her determination to generate pertinent data despite the pressures of time, equipment and lack of support. Shelly showed determination to not generate just any data, but data that was trustworthy, as shown by her frequent writing, erasure and rewriting of measurements.

For the children in *Place Value*, the safety of the tree provided many opportunities to *find* and to *generate* ideas that they could further explore. There is a sense that the 'finding' in this setting was expansive, in contrast with the classroom where the finding process came across as almost pedantic. Under the tree, some children moved from one activity to another, and you might call that 'exploration'. But in a classroom context, that same way of learning could be called 'unfocussed'. How did the children navigate affectively between these two learning worlds on a daily basis? Did the classroom learning partially impel students, by the time they were seven-year-olds, to play games with other people's rules—like volleyball? Or is the progression from unbounded play to play with boundaries just a natural part of childhood development? Where the affective domain for *find & generate* is taken to an extreme, it becomes *pedantic*; a deficit in this affect could be called *slapdash*.

Autonomy

The children in *Place Value* are again at opposite ends of the *learning autonomy* continuum when tree-based finding is compared with classroom-based finding. In the tree, what the children found was constrained only by what remained, what was grown and what had recently washed up, dropped down and blown in, and so the children improvised continuously in terms of *find & generate*. In the maths class, their finding was prescribed down to a precise location: the number on the left, which had a special value. In the classroom, there was no opportunity for the children to improvise on that convention, with the expectation by the teacher that they would emulate.

In *Parachute*, Katie emulated the teacher's protocol and generated data in keeping with prescribed learning autonomy. Shelly had some scaffolds set by the teacher, but also had a high degree of independence within those scaffolds, improvising the protocol to suit her questions and generating data as she went. Kevin innovated, with the freedom to determine which product information or application processes he needed to know about, including how he could get the silver fluoride safely overseas.

2.3.3 Evaluate & Reflect

Process	Affective dimension	Question
Evaluate & reflect	Discerning	What do we trust?

Detail: Students evaluate the credibility of sources, information, data and ideas, and through reflection make their own learning processes visible.

The process of finding information or generating data naturally leads to questions about the trustworthiness of that information or data. Should students believe others' information, including the teacher's, by default? A risk in the Information Age is that students may become gullible consumers of information, and so the educative process must include ways for students to learn to *evaluate*. Likewise, students should not by default trust their own ideas or data, but should *evaluate* these and reflect on the processes they use throughout their own learning, including self-reflection to determine their own potential biases.

In *Place Value*, after the children called out 'fourteen' in response to the written number 'forty-one', the teacher cued to students that there may be an error, by repeating the first part of the number: 'Four…'. A student then self-corrected with this prompting, calling the number 'fourteen'. When the class was prompted by the teacher to indicate whether the initial number sequence was correct, many students cried 'no', but no-one volunteered which number was incorrect until one girl standing in the line of eight students pointed at 'forty-one'. The teacher asked where 'forty-one' should go. Many children pointed to the next position up, so the teacher prompted the child holding 'forty-one' and the child holding 'seventeen' to shuffle and change places.

It is one thing to know what is wrong, and another thing to make it right. The evaluation process was incremental—students caused 'forty-one' to move to the right-hand side of seventeen, but not past twenty or twenty-nine. It may have been initially that the student holding the 'forty-one' saw it as 'fourteen', and so he was correct in sequencing it between nine and seventeen. But with the realisation that it was not fourteen but forty-one, there was no aspect that was correct in the sequence '17, 41, 20'. The salient aspect for *evaluate* is that the teacher prioritised evaluative thinking by allowing the class to place forty-one incorrectly, knowing the continuation of the exercise allowed for further correction. In other words, the teacher's Socratic questioning focused on the process of evaluation, not on getting the correct answer. This approach can take some of the fear out of learning, if students can incrementally correct rather than being corrected first-off. The teacher could also have asked for reflection at the end of that task: 'What was one number that started in the wrong place and now is in the right place?' and 'What is more important—that we got it right the first time, or got it right in the end?' In that way, she would have been helping students learn to be evaluative and reflective.

Kevin had to decide whether the silver fluoride's negatives (such as staining of teeth) were outweighed by the positives of tooth decay prevention. With this in mind, his cost–benefit analysis for potential patients in Cambodia would be very different from a cost–benefit analysis for urban dwellers in a developed nation. This is because evaluation is context-sensitive, and in this case determined by cultural and social factors, as well as by medical and economic ones.

In *Parachute*, Shelly engaged in evaluative thinking, measuring, writing, erasing, re-measuring, rewriting and erasing numbers that represented her measured drop times. When Mrs Breen asked, 'Did you use several measurements?' she was getting at the underlying repeatability of measurements in science, not relying on a single measure. This is a kind of incremental approach towards a 'true' value, where random errors decrease as the number of measurements increases. Shelly answered 'yes' truthfully. And with her repeated rubbing-out of numbers, she indicated a dissatisfaction with some of her measurements—an evaluative decision in which she was being discerning. Perhaps this is because she realised a problem with the measurement, such as stopping her timer too early or starting too late, or that the parachute didn't fully open. If that was the case, she was engaging in an evaluative search for accurate measurements. It is also possible that she knew that measurements shouldn't be too spread out, which would indicate a lack of precision, and she wanted to eliminate some recorded numbers that made her experiment seem to lack quality. Given the rushed timeframe, whether she was evaluating the measures themselves, or the appearance of her experiment, she demonstrated a high level of evaluative thinking.

Nevertheless, it was Shelly's evaluative thinking in *Parachute* that shocked me. How could a series of maths calculations leave her to critique not the actual numbers she obtained, but the shortfall of materials ('there isn't enough')? In the complexities of a genuinely open inquiry, where Shelly autonomously determined independent, dependent and key-controlled variables, she failed to make an absolutely vital evaluation of size. She seemed to believe that her hand-sized circle would be matched in the area by a square bigger than her desk. Ultimately, she applied a wrong maths formula—perimeter of a square instead of area of a square—but one would hope the discrepancy would have been enough for Shelly to stop and think that there must be a calculation error. This did not happen without intervention.

Affect: Discerning

Place Value's maths lesson required students to be discerning, requiring more than the evaluative element discussed earlier. Rather it was epitomised by the student who took a risk and pointed at the incorrect number—a willingness to question and maybe break through a group silence. Without this willingness, the teacher would have been left merely telling the group what was wrong, or the group would have been stuck with incorrect ideas.

Shelly was brave and smart in her parachute experiment. She was pressed for time because she chose to do what the teacher really wanted—her own investigation rather than what was modelled as an example. Everything had to be thought through, quickly, in eighty minutes minus the teacher's talk, making Shelly's task seriously complicated. In this case, she was asked to reflect on her learning: 'list what went wrong, and how you could improve', but Shelly had no time to work on that before she submitted her report. That was an opportunity missed, for her reflections on the eighty minutes may have taught her much. Shelly showed herself to be discerning, for example, by reporting only the positive aspects of her experiment when the teacher asked her how she was going, and through her willingness to erase and re-measure even under extreme time pressures. However, she did not see the size discrepancy resulting from her maths calculations for square size was a major concern.

Being discerning is vital for tree climbing; you have to avoid stepping onto a thin or dead branch that can't hold your weight, in effect asking each time 'is this branch strong enough?' with a compelling motivation to get this evaluative question right. The six-year-olds under the tree had no time pressure: if they were finding similar items, they could use any selection criteria for any feature they liked: species, colour, size, shape—there was no specific curriculum, and the exercise was self-correcting. Did they learn through outside play to be more evaluative or more reflective than in the classroom? For example, asking 'is this seed safe to eat?' is a very practical and natural question that fosters children to become discerning. Similarly, working without externally imposed boundaries, Kevin needed to be creatively discerning, projecting himself into an unfamiliar context, in effect asking himself before travelling 'will silver fluoride cause problems with and for villagers in Cambodia?'

Autonomy

Shelly sought for help, but only because she evaluated the plastic as too small to make a large-enough square. She self-evaluated many components of her work, especially the quality of data, by measuring, recording, erasing and re-measuring, and was mainly working at an *initiating* level of autonomy, even ignoring the teacher's request for reflection on the process. The children in *Place Value* were probed with Socratic questioning by their teacher to structure their thinking at the bounded level, in order to enable their group evaluation. At times, one student's evaluation became a modelling for the others. The activity was more bounded than prescribed, because students had several options when choosing what number was in the wrong place, and then several options for where to move the numbers. Nevertheless, most students showed evidence of emulating the teacher or experienced peers in terms of evaluation, with only a few students improvising. Kevin's own evaluative standards (prevention of decay) and his decision to intentionally disregard certain criteria (aesthetics) all emerged from his innovation and sensitivity to the context.

2.3.4   *Organise & Manage*

Process	Affective dimension	Question
Organise & manage	Harmonising	How do we arrange?

Detail: Students *organise* information & data to reveal patterns/themes and *manage* teams and processes.

To *organise* information is to enable its effective use. Where there is a plethora of information and data, organisational processes and formats help to enable sophisticated thinking, especially analyses. Written, spoken and graphical conventions for organising information and data enable subject-appropriate ways of communicating. The management of resources (both physical and electronic), of people in teams and of time all strongly influence how sophisticated student thinking may become.

The children in and around the tree in *Place Value* played until after sunset, doing whatever they wanted in that timeframe. Learning wasn't pre-planned; it was managed by them—they organised their time, equipment, spatial arrangement and the things they found. They could be up the tree, under the tree, or indeed anywhere else, but perhaps something communal kept them within six metres of each other.

In the maths class, by stark contrast, there was strict management of the students: the bell would ring one hour after recess; the teacher determined the time allocated to whole-class tasks and then individual tasks; the space was teacher determined, whether on the Pacific Island *italitali* mat, standing in a line in front of the class or at individual desks. The tasks required pre-specified ways of organising the whole class and individual activities. Organisation and management, as dictated by the teacher, were directed towards achieving as much learning about place value as possible. But how often were the students aware of teacher modelling and their own use of managing and organising skills?

Shelly's experience was closer to that of the children when they played outside than their experience in the maths lesson. While she had about the same amount of time as the six-year-olds in the classroom, between the teacher explanations, clarifications and requirements, she had to determine exactly how to manage herself and the experiment. For some aspects of organising the information, Shelly followed a standardised structure that she had used before: title, aim, results, with observation table and bar graph, and conclusion. However, for the table and graph, she had to *organise* the data by determining what the table comprised, identifying the x-axis and y-axis components of the graph, which required a degree of difficulty much higher than previous work, and all in a rushed timeframe.

Kevin had to work out the constraints of international travel and the village situation himself, and that these constraints would determine what he could carry and what he could manage to do. This included weight limits, knowing what goods could be imported to Cambodia, and the equipment available. Every aspect of *organise & manage* he determined and *initiated*.

Affect

Organise & manage can appear the least affective-oriented facet, but if students find the whole learning process under-stimulating, tedious or overly complex, then potential learning gains may not eventuate, no matter the learning design used. Einstein urged 'Out of clutter, find simplicity. From discord, find harmony' [25]. Organising cluttered information and managing discord requires an affective element: *harmonising*. This affective element addresses the question, 'how do we arrange?' How do we take cluttered, incoherent data or information and harmonise it in ways that enable effective analysis? How do we manage our team to work harmoniously? In *Place Value*, there are harmonious arrangements, with the children playing individually and yet socially in the shared tree-space. The highly prescribed maths lesson presents the harmonies of children on a pacific island mat chanting and learning together with the teacher. By calling out eight children to the front of the class, rather than individuals, the teacher managed the class harmoniously in the context of the cultural setting.

In *Parachute*, the time pressures brought discord to Shelly's open-ended experimentation, while Katie's prescribed experiment was relaxed. Even if Shelly learned more, what lesson did she walk away with? Given her level of anxiety, would her learning in this lesson have been less about experimental design and more about planning future work in which she could *emulate* the teacher's example, like other students?

Kevin was endeavouring to tread a fine line between the help that he hoped to give and the actual helpfulness of his planning, knowing that success would depend on how people in Cambodian villages actually reacted to stained teeth. That he used the silver fluoride a lot when he was over there suggests that he began by anticipating a high demand for the product, that he took a lot of it with him, and that this harmonised with the reality of what the Cambodians in villages were willing to do to protect their teeth.

Autonomy

Shelly struggled to squeeze her self-determined experiment into the 80 min allocated to the lesson. Her time management was paramount, and at one point she created for herself a resource management issue that didn't exist: she decided that she didn't have enough material. She then spent time talking to me, trying to source more plastic. Simultaneously, she was organising data into tables and graphs that reflected her actual fields (time and shape) and measurements of time. Shelly *improvised* organisational structures because not all options were fully open. For example, she was provided with the structure of 'aim, method, results and conclusion', and was aware that her teacher would mark her work according to (unknown?) criteria after the class. But Shelly managed this experimental process amazingly well, to the extent that she did finish and submit, albeit without the self-reflective part that her teacher requested near the end of the vignette.

Manage & Organise were highly structured in the *Place Value* classroom, with student bodily emulation of the teacher's physical management. Innovation was epitomised by the students by the seashore and by Kevin.

2.3.5 Analyse & Synthesise

Process	Affective dimension	Question
Analyse & synthesise	Creative	What does it mean?

Details: Students *analyse* information/data critically and *synthesise* new knowledge to produce coherent individual/team understandings.

Analysis involves the complexities of breaking things down into their constituent parts and bringing them back together in a way that enables trends (in quantitative work) and themes (in qualitative work) to become evident. There is, then, a strong, recursive interaction between *organise* and *analyse*, through determining how information and data may be arranged to enable insight into what words, numbers, icons and other representations mean. Synthesis is the process of creating something new from all the constituent parts. At the most fundamental level, this entails an individual's construction of understanding, or a team's construction of understanding. Understanding may be manifest in all sorts of physical and digital representations, from essays to multimedia mash-ups. While 'understanding' is the second-from-bottom taxon in Bloom's Taxonomy of the Cognitive Domain, in MELT it emerges non-sequentially, and in some ways is a culmination of sophisticated learning.

When students *analyse & synthesise* others' information along with their own prior knowledge, they construct understanding new to themselves in a process that often involves creativity, or the creation of something new. Synthesis happens in the context of students' prior knowledge. In *Place Value*, the lesson focus is on the value associated with the 'place' of a numeral in a two-digit number. Single-digit numbers are relatively concrete, but a number represented by two or more numerals is a substantial abstraction. Without an understanding of the value attributed to a specific place (e.g. that the left-hand number in a two-digit numeral indicates the number of groups of ten, and the right-hand number indicates the number of units), students can make few conceptual advances in our decimal system of mathematics.

So, from the start of this activity in *Place Value*, there may have been some maths anxiety, especially given that English was the second language for all the students, so that their familiarity with number names would have been lower than if English was their mother tongue.

Whilst we saw in Sect. 2.3.3 that the six-year-olds evaluated 'forty-one' as being in the wrong place, this didn't automatically entail that they could locate the *right* place for the number. The students seemed to have trouble seeing the trend in numbers as a whole and being able to place forty-one correctly after twenty-nine—in other words, they struggled to *analyse*.

The teacher asked a question that seemed practical, but which actually required analytical thinking. It was not a question which merely evaluated whether forty-one was in an incorrect position; it also asked students to project the number to its proper place: 'So this forty-one should go *where*?' For students to see the numerical trend, to show analytical thinking, they needed to move forty-one up three places in the line. However, the students indicated that it should go past seventeen only, and the boy with forty-one moved up one place: '5, 9, 11, 17, **41**, 20, 29, 57'.

If the process of evaluating forty-one's position continued incrementally 'it's wrong here.... It's wrong here, ah, it's correct here', then it would have been a trial and error process. This would be similar to (but more sophisticated than) the evaluative thinking required to check whether a square peg fit into a round hole, and then trying each subsequent hole until it fits. The teacher knew that forty-one was still in the wrong place, but demonstrated pedagogical awareness that if she kept on asking 'are you sure?' regarding forty-one specifically, she would be cuing that forty-one *was* wrongly placed. Such a strategy may not even facilitate evaluative thinking; it would merely train students to read the teacher's cues.

The teacher instead asked, 'Any *other* number is in the wrong place?' Here, she shifted the class focus from forty-one, towards looking at all the numbers afresh and analysing the trend. One student evaluated 'twenty-nine' as being in the wrong place. The teacher then asked a question about twenty-nine, the same question she asked about forty-one. Again, in this context, this could have represented an attempt to elicit analytical thinking: 'Twenty-nine should go where?'

'Besides seventeen' one student called out—and the student with twenty-nine shuffled left, passing forty-one and twenty '5, 9, 11, 17, **29**, **41**, 20, 57.

Indeed, this was the first time a student required a number to move two places at once, and downstream at that. This one student had seen something in the trend (e.g., his internal reasoning may have been something like 'twenty-nine is lower than forty-one and higher than seventeen, so it should go between these two numbers'). This process of seeing the trend rather than engaging in evaluative trial and error indicates analytical reasoning. The sequence as yet was not perfected, but the student's request represented a major leap forward, from an incremental, evaluative process to a more analytical one. The other students could see and hear this, and realised that they too could do more than say 'not here'—instead, they could project a number into its correct location in the sequence. That leap of two places was a leap of insight for the child, and may have triggered some new ways of thinking for other children.

Still, it is hard to see errors, let alone trends in numbers, and when the teacher asked if there was any other number in the wrong place, the students called out together, 'No'. It may seem bewildering that thirty-one bright students 'missed' the '20', especially after another number in the twenties (twenty-nine) was just moved.

'Are you sure?' she presses.
'Twenty!' a boy calls out
'Right.' Where should it go?
'Besides seventeen'

Again, this child's analysis went beyond seeing that twenty was in the wrong position, into spotting the trend and placing the number in its correct place.

The students' process suggested that some of the students could *evaluate*, on a case-by-case basis, whether a number was in the right or the wrong position. But to *analyse* entailed being able to move a number to its correct position, even if this required big jumps. At the end of the activity, there were now two students who showed evidence of being analytical, and they modelled this ability to the class.

In *Parachute*, Shelly worked out that there was a difference in parachute drop times, and since she had controlled other factors, she inferred that the difference was due to the parachute's shape. She stated to Mrs Breen that 'the round one takes longer to hit the ground.' To reach this analysis, Shelly shifted from one particular observation ('the round parachute in each drop took longer') to a generalisation ('the round one [always] takes longer'). For her conclusion, she elaborated on that analysis to form a full synthesis of her previous and current understanding of the nature of science experiments, and of the analysis she conducted, to say, 'If the key factors are the same the parachute should come down at the same rate'. Because square versus round parachutes didn't have the same drop time, she synthesised her conclusion as a generalisation: 'the shape does matter to the time'. The finding that drop time depended on parachute shape represented a substantial synthesis of empirically based understanding, developed in an eighty-minute lesson by a thirteen-year-old student.

Kevin's analysis included a conscious consideration of social, cultural and contextual issues, in order to determine whether he was right in thinking that silver fluoride may have been appropriate. There was also a technical side to his analysis—e.g., 'how poisonous is silver fluoride if ingested, or if it makes contact with skin?' His analysis may not have stretched to 'how sustainable will this approach be for each village?' His final synthesis included the decision to take the compound, as well as considerations on how much to take, and how he would store it while travelling and when in the villages.

Affect: Creative

The *Place Value* maths activity was social, but frequently depended on an individual to go against the consensus and call out an error. This may have meant that some students who either saw a wrongly placed number, or who even saw where that number should go may have been inhibited to say so, perhaps because of cultural norms. The analytical learning evident in this activity seemed to rely on brave or confident individuals. To understand deeply what 'place value' meant, students had to be intuitive; students who were cognitively and affectively engaged in the task had to be very creative to move from their original understanding to a newly constructed understanding of the concept. This creativity was evidenced in the leap of imagination required for one student to send one number multiple places downstream. Three students from the class showed the creativity to conjure up different games from scratch each day as they played by the seashore. Shelly's analysis followed a scientific protocol, but she creatively adapted it to her parachute experiment. Kevin showed the creativity needed to think outside the content box of his study program. This allowed him to consider, from a raft of potential contributions, what he could add to oral health practice in a rural context.

Autonomy

In the *Place Value* maths lesson, the students' analysis and synthesis were scaffolded by the teacher, who put structures in place to help students *analyse* the numerical trend and rearrange the numbers into their correct order. For some or most students, this was too big a step. In the process, there was no modelling from the teacher. But the teacher scaffolded the task so that students modelled to other students the process of analytical thinking. Such peer-to-peer modelling was envisaged by Vygotsky in the ZPD, and peer teaching is often regarded as more conducive to student learning than teacher talk [26].

Kevin's *initiation* of analysis was unbounded by any supervisory presence, but this unboundedness didn't mean 'anything goes'. This was especially true in terms of his patients' health, which was in his silver fluoride-laden hands. If Kevin, for example, ignored or overlooked a health warning, he may have endangered his patients. If applied inexpertly, the treatment may have been ineffective or counterproductive. Even though Kevin may have been working outside the boundaries of a specific health system, his status as a professional required him to be aware of how 'unbounded' his work was, and therefore to redouble caution, checking and rechecking dosages.

Shelly *initiated* her own *analysis & synthesis* and this was in keeping with the teacher's more open-ended intention, and so the teacher had no preconceived answer for Shelly's self-generated question. The teacher could check the process and the steps which Shelly used to get to her conclusion, but could not rightly correct the findings themselves.

2.3.6   Communicate & Apply

Process	Affective dimension	Question
Communicate & apply	Constructive	How do we relate?

Detail: Students *apply* their understanding and *discuss, listen, write, perform, respond to feedback* and *present* processes, knowledge and implications while heeding *ethical, cultural, social and team* (ECST) issues and audience needs.

Communication frequently is thought of in terms of written, spoken, multimedia and performance *products* for an audience, and application is thought to concern built solutions to a problem. However, like all the facets, *communicate* and *apply* are primarily *processes* that students engage in during sophisticated thinking, even though they may also comprise final outputs. Students begin by applying their prior knowledge to a task, and as they develop understanding, they apply that new understanding to their task. The communication process has many aspects, and involves more than speaking and writing—it also entails listening, reading, performing and responding to feedback. In the process of applying this facet, ethical, cultural, social and team (ECST) elements need to be emphasised, as mentioned for *embark & clarify*.

Whilst they seemed to be involved in individual agendas when I watched them playing around the tree, the children in *Place Value* were vocalising the whole time. Whether they were chatting, gibbering or explicitly communicating with each other, I couldn't tell. Although they were each doing different things, the proximity of the six children to each other was striking; they were together in individual ways. The three- to six-year-olds acted out the facet 'apply' through the use of their existing knowledge and turning their thoughts to their environment—was there something there which they didn't know about, or suddenly thought differently about? Would they apply their maths to counting objects? Would they arrange things on the mat in ways they had seen others do in a shop setting? Or would they just bounce in a branch, and somehow learn about natural rhythms, about the properties of living wood, of the texture of bark, and develop tacit knowledge of how to grip a moving branch?

In the village, many coconuts were harvested when green, a long time before they fell naturally, and so the village relied on good climbers. The boys in the village told me they could not climb a coconut tree until they were older than twelve—it required skill with a machete and upper body strength. But did climbing in the tree by the water provide a raft of knowledge and skills that could be applied later to climbing coconut trees?

The next day in the maths class, the teacher's use of a Pacific Island mat, the *italitali*, culturally affirmed the children's place in the Pacific. The communication between students was initially communal, with students chanting together and periodically falling into shared silence. When the eight students were allocated their numbers, they read them, and used the information of the two single-digit and six double-digit numbers to order themselves into a sequence. They used a lot of whispering and pointing, pushing and shuffling to end up with a communication product—their sequence of numbers—reached by consensus, under time pressure and maybe stage-fright. Standing there in their sequence, they hoped to *communicate* visually, holding numbers so that they were visible to the twenty-three others who remained on the *italitali* mat. Therefore, the group was exposed to critique because their communication was in plain sight and open to a form of peer-review. That the sequence was constructed by a group of students reduced potential feelings of exposure when compared, say, to an individual sequencing numbers on a whiteboard. Nevertheless, the eight students and their thinking were exposed. Students on the mat scanned the sequence time and again, and endeavoured to *communicate* through silence, speaking or pointing their answer in response to the teacher's communication prompt, 'is there any number in the wrong place?' This evaluative question prompted students to answer with something specific, in contrast to a vaguer question, such as 'is this sequence correct?'

Maybe it's to be expected that the student who first communicated an answer to this question was engaged in the process of forming the sequence, rather than sitting passively on the mat. When number five pointed to forty-one, she broke the stillness which had suggested collective acquiescence regarding the correctness of the existing sequence. The student holding 'five' did not just *evaluate* the sequence and diagnose that it was wrong, but actively indicated through pointing and speaking which number in the sequence was incorrect. Once challenged, the class began to agree with her, and in that way, her communication broke a silence. Once the silence was broken, individual students worked up the courage to start challenging class consensus, and this moved the community forward towards the correct sequence. Once forty-one was challenged, students had to apply their knowledge to suggest *where* forty-one should go. After this, many students communicated by pointing, as if vocalising a specific place was too difficult or risky. The standing, pointing and shuffling made embodied communication the number one communication mode in the class. It was this form of communication that enabled some students to apply their knowledge of two-digit numbers.

In *Parachute*, Shelly wrote in her report,

> If the key factors are the same the parachute should come down at the same rate as it was not proven here I have come to the conclusion that the shape does matter to the time.

This excerpt is cryptic at first glance. But it closely follows the 'null hypothesis' strategy used commonly in science, whereby scientists try to show that there is no statistical difference, after which the discovery of a difference indicates that there must be a genuine difference in effect due to the independent variable. Shelly merely took averages, which are very weak descriptive statistics. Nevertheless, she adopted the persuasive grammatical structures of science to *communicate* in writing. However, she had made a similar point earlier when talking to Mrs Breen, in a way that was much easier to understand: 'the round one takes longer to hit the ground.' The report is much more science-speak than her oral communication, and as her main communication product, the report goes beyond communicating results and demonstrates her findings using scientific discourse. In choosing a communication style that was appropriate to the situation, Shelly did something that is vital in all learning contexts. The fact that different styles and modes are required in different settings suggests that 'communication' is not a singular skill. Rather, it comes in multiple forms, each of which must be learned and incorporated into a personal repository of styles to be drawn-upon as context demands.

When Kevin communicated with Cambodians in the village, he wanted them to have confidence that what he was offering would work. But his audience may not have wanted or understood a scientific discourse. In this situation, *apply* may have seemed more important to Kevin than *communicate*: 'I thought that might be really beneficial for Cambodia because they don't get care often.' He wanted and found something that worked, and was driven to be constructive, to build up. He anticipated linguistic barriers, but knew that the care he could give would speak volumes.

For Kevin, communication included a willingness to listen to someone with an experience that differed from his, someone with rural experience, and this included practice that was contrary to standard practice in his degree. He used the silver fluoride 'a lot over there', implying that he persuaded people in the village to tolerate stained teeth in order to keep their teeth longer. Clearly, his intention was to be constructive. This is where the ethical, cultural and social dimensions really kick in. He applied the idea of silver fluoride, evaluated his use of it with people and decided to continue to use it a lot. Communication and application were a type of endpoint for his sophisticated thinking. But they are also a part of the process from the beginning, including listening, finding out what was currently available and what was applicable.

Affect: Constructive

The default affective adjective in MELT for this facet is *constructive*, used in the colloquial sense of 'you're a constructive person' or 'that's a constructive comment'. A constructive student or graduate desires to build up rather than self-promote in their applications and communications. Shelly endeavoured to not only be intrepid, but to craft a quality finding.

Kevin was a constructive graduate who volunteered, prepared and purchased equipment using his own money, well in advance. He communicated and maybe persuaded as he went, and applied his knowledge with the intention to add value to the lives of people who were otherwise unreached by dental services. In doing so, he personified the end-game of research and problem-solving: 'go to where the silence is and say something' [27]. Of course, it may be that having committed to silver fluoride, Kevin was doggedly committed to use it or get rid of it. There is the possibility that he foisted the product on a more vulnerable population, over-riding their aesthetic concerns. Kevin, and each of us, ethically and culturally must prioritise others and not use coercion to peddle wares or to enforce our own values, like a mini-colonisation.

The children in *Place Value* were preoccupied with play in the tree, and in that setting they entertained themselves without needing any adult resources. The eight children in line applied their understanding of place value and communicated this to the whole class. Their willingness to do this and to be critiqued enabled an entire constructive dialogue to be engineered by the teacher.

Autonomy

That communicative line-up in *Place Value* had predetermined boundaries, and even with one ultimate correct answer, the scope was there for incremental improvement. Giving the children some room to move enabled substantial learning. Kevin and the children under the tree had unbounded autonomy to *communicate* and *apply*. Shelly faced a mixed bag, with the prescribed structure of a lab write-up and her own innovations to report, whereas Katie stayed within the modelling provided, successfully *emulating* the teachers' lead.

2.3.7 Spiralling, Recursive and Messy

Sections 2.3.1–2.3.6 are arranged in a logical and coherent order and present as a more linear representation of the MELT facets. However, the reality of sophisticated learning is that it is messier than a sequence. At times, several facets occur simultaneously, or facets like *evaluate* and *reflect* are tightly coupled to every other facet. Simultaneously, purpose drives everything, frequently requiring a return to *embark & clarify*. It is to capture the non-sequential nature of sophisticated learning that MELT uses the word *facet:* It's as if there are six faces of one precious learning jewel, where different facets are emphasised depending on which way one holds the jewel, yet all co-exist simultaneously.

There are different practical ways that facets may interconnect or be emphasised in MELT. The ethical, cultural, social and team considerations are evident in *embark & clarify* and in *communicate & apply*, and as noted earlier this is the only repeated element in the explicit articulations of MELT. This double-mention was seen to be an essential emphasis that needed to be articulated explicitly in those *facets* often seen at the beginning and end of engaged learning. However, when students think in ways that are sophisticated for them, all *facets* are enacted continuously throughout the whole process. Most noticeably this occurs with *evaluate*, where questions, information, management and communication are always evaluated, or should be, and at times analysis is inseparable from evaluative process. The pentagon formulation of MELT also urges 'when in doubt, return to the centre' to *embark & clarify* 'what is our purpose?' This acknowledges the recursive, messy aspects of sophisticated thinking and the strong need for learner clarity, or more precisely, for learners to develop clarity of purpose. However, Chap. 3 provides examples where educators use the pentagon configuration and place one of the other five MELT facets in the centre, and this matches their emphasis for sophisticated thinking.

The cognitive and affective are not separated in MELT in the way that they were in Bloom's taxonomies. Separating these two sides of the same *facet* can provide a licence to prioritise one over the other. However, a challenge of modern education is to 'cover' the essential knowledge and skills for contemporary life, but in a way that provides at least enough motivation for students to acquire these, a challenge that requires simultaneous cognitive and affective considerations. I suggest that the above sections unpack some of the complexities of the processes in each story and account, and as educators, one of our challenges is to understand the complexity for students of affectively engaging in sophisticated learning. In all of the research on MELT implementation to date, student need and employ all six facets in activities that require anything more than dialogic-reproductive learning, and that such learning is always multifaceted needs further research. If the facets of MELT are not explicitly facilitated, at appropriate times, then the risk is under-developed student thinking being applied across the years of education. Therefore, another challenge is to facilitate the development of all of the facets that students need, in consideration of context, content knowledge and diversity of learners.

In Sect. 2.2, the more cognitive descriptions of MELT were co-presented with the un-elaborated affective domain, for these dimensions of learning mutually reinforce and co-exist. When designing any learning tasks (including assessment), educators need to consider affect, so that motivational elements in learning tasks are integral to curriculum and lesson design. But this does not mean the affective domain needs to be assessed, and the MELT's single-word affect descriptors are a type of warning: don't treat the affective domain in the same way as the cognitive domain. The affective domain is crucial because it is salient to ethical, cultural and social considerations for engaged teaching and learning.

As with all MELT terminology, the affective adjectives are context-sensitive, and should readily be adapted by educators to fit that context. For example, *curious* may be, at times, a word that is contrary to ethical and moral imperatives, and a word like *empathetic* may be more appropriate in the context of solving people's problems or dealing with patients. Kevin may have been curious to see if silver fluoride was effective, but hopefully his primary driver was empathy for people who had minimal access to dental care. In applying the affective descriptor for *communicate & apply—constructive*—it is important to pay heed to ethical and cultural issues. Some people may feel that 'constructive' contains overtones of colonisation, echoing Rome's mission to 'civilise' the world. In being *constructive*, one should avoid foisting one's own solutions or morals onto others; the ECST considerations are designed to check such impulses. If Kevin's silver fluoride solution proved to be socially or culturally inappropriate when he was in a village, he would need to heed this rather than persuading people with a medicine-only orientation, while defending himself as being *constructive*.

2.4 Conclusion: Engagement, Adaptability, Fluidity and Ownership

My operational definition of engagement is 'frequently socially interactive and always minds-on', and the six facets of MELT require engaged learners and engaged teachers. The shared conceptualisation afforded by MELT can broaden the community of people who are involved in using and discussing the models, making conversations richer: Librarians, casual staff, principals, museum directors, office staff, assistant lecturers, professors, parents and caregivers can be enjoined in conversations with teachers and students, whatever the years and focus of study.

However, a shared conceptualisation does not necessitate shared terminology, and adaptations to MELT are in the spirit of the models' broad parameters. Adaptation from a general description to context-sensitive applications is vital. At times, one context, such as a school or a university program, may require several different MELT that express core ideas in different ways. The challenge, then, is to help students realise that there is just one shared model at work, to help them make the connections between the different models, and to see how to generalise their own learning as a whole. All of this is part of building and internalising their own personal models of learning, which will become a thinking routine that can guide them across their education.

Chapter 3 contains diverse examples of the explicit use of MELT. These examples demonstrate how different groups have taken the ideas presented here, adapted them and used them to help students understand what is going on in their learning. This level of fluidity is liberating and demanding. As MELT is not a generic model that guarantees effective learning through an off-the-shelf solution, but rather requires significant input to reformulate and re-articulate, it places demands on teachers. This is why the examples in Chap. 3 are so helpful: there is no need to re-invent the wheel if you can find and adapt from contexts close to yours. Educators making choices on how to adapt MELT to fit specific contexts and what to emphasise have a liberty that defers to their professional judgement. However, they cannot ignore that we all need to be better informed about how to enable sophisticated, multifaceted thinking.

References

1. Einstein Bubble in Cartoon: Bucky, P., Einstein, A., & Weakland, A. (1992). *The private Albert Einstein*. Kansas City, Missouri: Andrews and McMeel.
2. Willison, J. W., & O'Regan, K. (2005). 2020 Vision: An information literacy continuum for students primary to postgraduation. In *Research and development in higher education: Proceedings of the higher education research and development conference*. Sydney, 3–6 July, 2005.
3. Bundy, A. (Ed.). (2004). *Australian and New Zealand Information Literacy framework: Principles, standards and practice* (5th ed.). Adelaide, Australia: Australian and New Zealand Institute for Information Literacy.
4. Biggs, J., & Collis, K. (1989). Towards a model of school-based curriculum development and assessment using the SOLO taxonomy. *Australian Journal of Education, 33*(2), 151–163.
5. Bloom, B. S. (1956). *Taxonomy of educational objectives. Vol. 1: Cognitive domain*. New York, NY: McKay.
6. Krathwohl, D. R, Bloom, B. S., & Masia, B. B. (1964). *Taxonomy of educational objectives. Vol. 2: Affective domain*. New York, NY: McKay.
7. Pring, R. (1971). Bloom's Taxonomy: A philosophical critique (2). *Cambridge Journal of Education, 1*(2), 83–91.
8. Willison, J., & O'Regan, K. (2007). Commonly known, commonly not known, totally unknown: A framework for students becoming researchers. *Higher Education Research and Development, 26*(4), 393–409.
9. Vygotsky, L. S. (1978). *Mind in society*. Cambridge, MA: Harvard University Press.
10. Willison, J., Sabir, F., & Thomas, J. (2017). Shifting dimensions of autonomy in students' research and employment. *Higher Education Research & Development, 36*(2), 430–443.
11. Willison, J., & O'Regan, K. (2005). 2020 Vision: An information literacy continuum for students primary school to post graduation. In *Proceedings from the HERDSA Conference*. Sydney, Australia: Higher Education Research and Development Society of Australasia. Retrieved from http://www.herdsa.org.au/publications/conference-proceedings/researchand-development-higher-education-higher-education-121.
12. Dewey, J. (1908). What does pragmatism mean by practical? *The Journal of Philosophy, Psychology and Scientific Methods, 5*(4), 85–99.
13. Hackling, M. W., & Fairbrother, R. W. (1996). Helping students to do open investigations in science. *Australian Science Teachers' Journal, 42*(4), 26–33.

14. Wood, D., Bruner, J. S., & Ross, G. (1976). The role of tutoring in problem solving. *Journal of Child Psychology and Psychiatry, 17*(2), 89–100.
15. Willison, J., Peirce, E., & Ricci, M. (2009). Towards student autonomy in literature and field research. In H. Wozniak, & S. Bartoluzzi (Eds.), *Proceedings of the Higher Education Research and Development Society of Australasia National Conference: The Student Experience* (pp. 483–491). Darwin, Australia: Higher Education Research and Development Society of Australasia. Retrieved from http://www.herdsa.org.au/publications/conference-proceedings/research-and-development-higher-education-student-experience-72.
16. Willison, J., Zhu, X., Xie, B., Yu, X., Chen, C., Zhang, D, Shashoug, I. & Sabir, F. (in press). Graduates' affective transfer of research skills and evidence based practice from university to employment in clinics. *BMC Medical Education*. https://digital.library.adelaide.edu.au/dspace/bitstream/2440/92390/3/hdl_92390.pdf
17. Harari, Y. N. (2018). *21 lessons for the 21st century*. New York, NY: Spiegel & Grau.
18. Seidenberg, A. (1961). The ritual origin of geometry. *Archive for History of Exact Sciences, 1*(5), 488–527.
19. Lyons, J. (2011). *The house of wisdom: How the Arabs transformed Western civilization*. New York, NY: Bloomsbury Publishing USA.
20. Crystal, Y. O., Janal, M. N., Hamilton, D. S., & Niederman, R. (2017). Parental perceptions and acceptance of silver diamine fluoride staining. *The Journal of the American Dental Association, 148*(7), 510–518.
21. Wilmore, M., & Willison, J. (2016). Graduates' attitudes to research skill development in undergraduate media education. *Asia Pacific Media Educator, 26*(1), 113–128.
22. Isaacson, W. (2007). *Einstein, his life and universe*. London, England: Simon and Schuster.
23. Crampon, J. E. (1988). Murphy, Parkinson, and Peter: Laws for libraries. *Library Journal, 113*(17), 37–41.
24. Chatterjee, H. J. (2010). Object-based learning in higher education: The pedagogical power of museums. *University Museums and Collections Journal, 3*, 79–81.
25. Brown, P. (1993). *Managing your time*. Cambridge: Daniels Publishing.
26. Casey, G. (2013). Building a student-centred learning framework using social software in the middle years classroom: An action research study. *Journal of Information Technology Education: Research, 12*, 159–189.
27. Goodman, A. (2010). Independent media in a time of war. *Sacred Heart University Review, 24*(1), 1.

Chapter 3:
How do we arrange?

Organise & Manage

HARMONISING

Chapter 3
How Do We Arrange?

One of the most common questions is 'how do others use the MELT?' When turning to the MELT, educators want more than a philosophy; they are looking for a framework that can give tangible starting points for facilitating sophisticated learning. This chapter provides examples of the ways that others have arranged MELT, to inspire educators to adapt the MELT to diverse contexts. Inspiration is provided through the diversity of contexts and approaches, rather than a narrow range of age- or content-specific resources.

Specifically, in this chapter shows how educators have used their own adaptations of the MELT to benefit student learning, with examples and links applicable to early childhood, primary, secondary, technical education, undergraduate, course-based master's, and doctoral programmes. There are also examples that span across disciplinary learning and transdisciplinary projects, and those that are aligned to Direct Instruction or to discovery learning.

In terms of modelling the MELT facets, they maybe taught and learned in the sequence presented in Chap. 2. However, in reality, sophisticated learning is frequently non-sequential, messy and recursive. A linear, sequential approach can be used early-on with students in highly prescriptive activities, and in contexts where they have little experience: this is the case whether in primary, middle and secondary school, undergraduate, Master's and sometimes the early months of Ph.D. studies. Once students can begin to make some decisions and display autonomy in their learning, they will employ the facets non-sequentially.

The figures below are screenshots of resources available online that are presented not to read in themselves, but to refer to the associated weblink.

© The Author(s) 2020
J. Willison, *The Models of Engaged Learning and Teaching*,
SpringerBriefs in Education, https://doi.org/10.1007/978-981-15-2683-1_3

3.1   MELT Connecting

MELT is applicable to many contexts. However, modifications necessary for MELT to work are needed for each context. Furthermore, how MELT should be implemented is determined by the specific contextual conditions. Only those individuals facilitating the learning have the requisite knowledge of the students, topics, desired learning outcomes and broader environment to make suitable professional judgements. For MELT to be effective, teacher engagement and autonomy are necessary.

To facilitate teacher engagement, experience and emerging evidence have demonstrated that the single most helpful factor for the successful adaptation and use of MELT is conversation. Through mature, inter-professional conversation, the MELT is defrosted and animated with the warmth of human interaction. These conversations may take place between colleagues, classroom teachers and coordinating academics, tutors at university, school and home, principals, librarians, learning advisors, and parents. Engagement, based around MELT, provides common ground and fosters discussions, collegial debate, disagreement, and ways to proceed. The most important conversations, however, are with and between students. A crucial pedagogical question is, 'when and to what extent should we make the MELT facets and the *continuum of autonomy* explicit so that students may metacognitively *follow, improvise* and *initiate*?'

3.2   Many Models Across Educational Levels and Contexts

For ease of access, the following sections are arranged according to educational levels. However, approaches used at one educational level maybe pertinent to other contexts. It is advisable to consider scanning several examples.

The approaches used are for:

- Early childhood—five-year-olds: song, rhythm and movement
- Year/Grade 4/5: problem-based learning pentagon for teacher planning
- Year/Grade 6: interactive introduction to investigation framework for direct student use in term-long projects, with issues chosen by students
- Year/Grade 7: interactive introduction to investigation framework for student direct use in guided transdisciplinary projects
- Year/Grade 8: interactive introduction to project-based learning pentagon for direct student use in an intensive three-week STEM project posed by an industry partner
- Year/Grade 9/10: interactive introduction to MELT for direct student use in three-term projects with issues chosen by students
- Technical and Further Education
- First year of university: interactive introduction to RSD and use across two consecutive terms; multiple assignments in terms of marking criteria and feedback
- Second year of university: Human Resource Management
- Honours year: Medical Science

- Master's year 1: interactive introduction to RSD and use across two consecutive assignments, in terms of marking criteria and feedback.
- Master's year 2: student self-assessment using RSD in the early phase of the major research project (one semester full-time)
- Doctoral studies: self and supervisor assessment of the proposal.

3.2.1 Early Childhood

Marsha Seebohm (a music specialist teacher at Elizabeth North Primary School in Adelaide) developed an exemplary tool for facilitating MELT in an early childhood education setting. In 2014, Marsha adapted MELT facets as lyrics to the tune of a widely-known folk song, 'She'll be coming 'round the mountain when she comes' so that it would be suitable for five-year-olds (Fig. 3.1).

Examples of children singing Research Mountain, and the actions associated with the song, performed by an adult audience are available on the MELT website. As a teaching tool, it is in keeping with the tenets of active, embodied learning which are so important in early childhood education contexts. Marsha developed the song to provide young students with a sung and performed heuristic for inquiry learning. She is exploring the song's use by teachers in their regular classes.

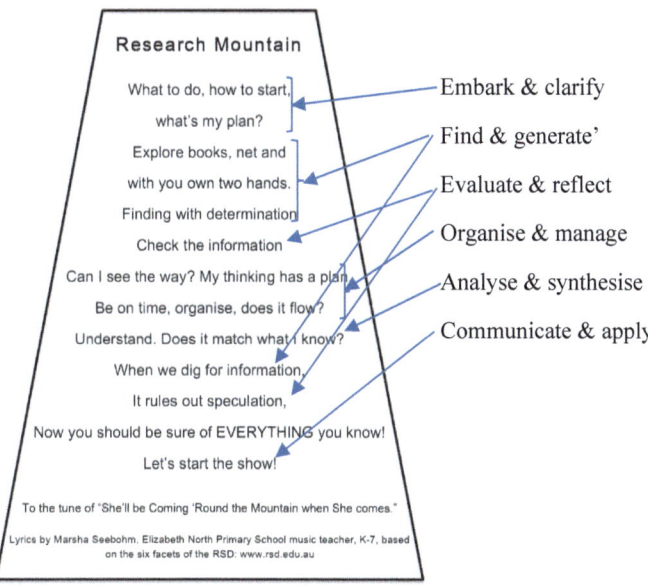

Fig. 3.1 Research mountain, a song for 5 year olds. https://www.adelaide.edu.au/melt/k-12-education#early-childhood

In addition to this example based on a folk song, another ECE version of MELT in action (based on a nursery rhyme) is on the website at www.melt.edu.au.

In this example, and some of the others below, there is no explicit mention of autonomy. Autonomy in these examples is an aspect for teachers who apply professional judgement in considering 'how much structure and guidance do these students need?' and whether to introduce ideas around autonomy or not.

3.2.2   Year 4/5 Primary

Year 4/5 teachers involved in a Science Technology Engineering and Maths (STEM) initiative at a government Primary School transformed the MELT into a Problem Solving Pentagon. The school had been introduced to an engineering design framework, the terminology of which was used to inform the Problem Solving Pentagon. The teachers used this for their own thinking about design in their lesson planning, but not explicitly to facilitate student learning. However, the motivation to develop the model was to facilitate student engagement in intentional learning in STEM (Fig. 3.2).

Fig. 3.2 Primary/elementary school problem-solving pentagon. www.adelaide. edu.au/melt/k-12-education# primary

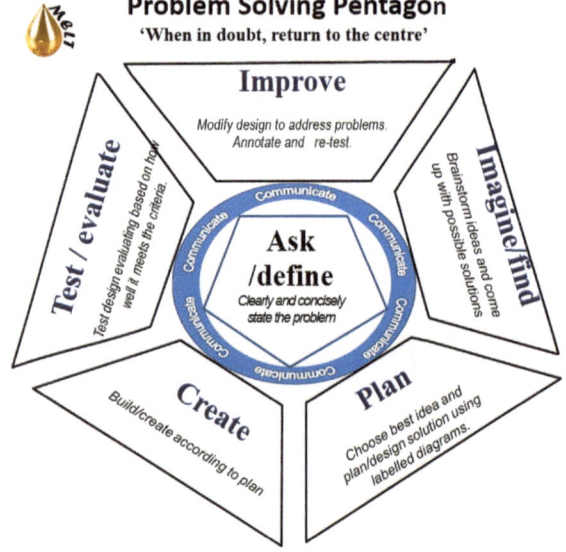

3.2.3 Year 6 Primary School

The International Baccalaureate (IB) is a curriculum that is run in many countries, with separate but related primary years, middle years and diploma (senior years) programmes. The Primary Years Programme (PYP) of the IB involves a major student exhibition. This exhibition provides the opportunity for students in Year/Grade 6 to engage in sustained project-based learning for a full term, and then present their discoveries at a public presentation. Likewise, the Middle Years Programme (MYP) personal project is a major piece of work spanning around three school terms. In the exhibition and the personal project, students provide evidence of their 'approaches to learning' (ATL), which comprises ten major elements that span PYP, MYP and the Diploma Programme (Table 3.1).

MELT facets directly connect to the ATL, so I ran IB teacher professional development sessions that focused on the use of the MELT pentagon as a way that students and teachers could engage directly with ATL. Students in government and non-government schools in three Australian states and New Zealand used MELT to plan out the beginning of their exhibition (Year 6) or personal project (Year 9/10). There was a demand for these sessions because schools identified the beginning phase of research in the Exhibition and the Personal Project to be a conceptual challenge that was, at times, daunting. Teacher Professional Development on MELT in the IB was provided on school sites and in state associations. These MELT workshops were

Table 3.1 The international baccelaureate's approaches to learning, mapped onto the MELT facets (see www.wcpss.net/Page/15023)

Approaches To learning	MELT facet
Collaboration skills	Explicitly mentioned in *embark & clarify*, *organise & manage*, *analyse & synthesise*, and *communicate & apply*
Communication skills	*Communicate & apply*
Organisation	*Organise & manage*
Reflection	*Evaluate & reflect*
Information literacy	The six facets of MELT are based on six Information Literacy Standards []
Critical thinking	The six facets, modified as appropriate, represent the breadth of critical thinking
Media literacy	The six facets, modified as appropriate, represent the breadth of media literacy
Affective	Each facet has an affective component that is integral
Creative thinking	'Creative' is positioned as an affective side to 'analyse and synthesise'
Transfer	'Apply' overlaps with this

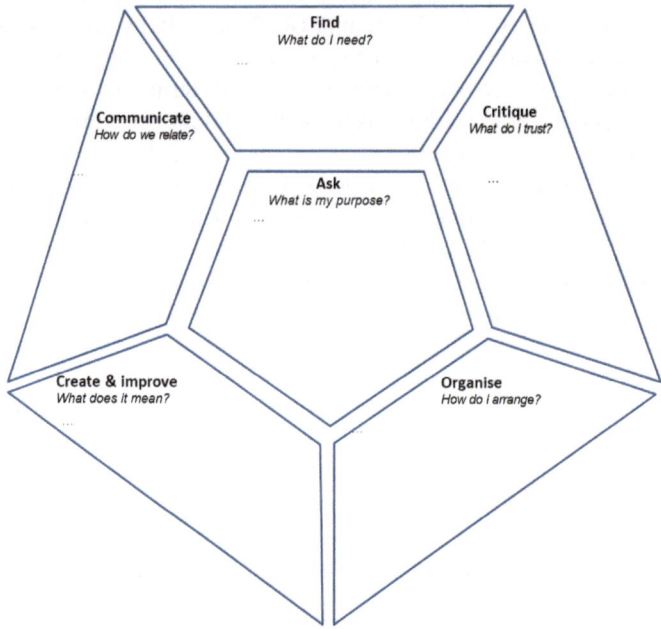

Inquiry Framework (IF?)

'When in doubt, return to the centre'

Find
What do I need?

Communicate
How do we relate?

Critique
What do I trust?

Ask
What is my purpose?

Create & improve
What does it mean?

Organise
How do I arrange?

Fig. 3.3 The Inquiry framework (IF), used directly with Year 6 students, so they can improve their understanding of their learning and communicate their reflective thinking. https://www.adelaide.edu.au/melt/k-12-education#primary

requested to better assist students to directly engage with, and become increasingly aware of, their own approaches to learning and how to represent that learning in an assessable 'Process Journal' (Fig. 3.3).

3.2.4 Year 8 Subject-Specific: *A Case Study*

High School specific resources are available at https://www.adelaide.edu.au/melt/k-12-education#secondary

A specific set of resources for high school is called *writE science* (Writing and Reading Integrated with Talking about Experiments) which integrates a MELT framework developed for Year 8 Science and presents explicit ways of developing the facets. *WritE* science has been used to inspire otherwise uninterested students to engage in hands-on labs to foster literacy—reading and writing. In effect, the strategy provides a platform where an individual student's preferences and strengths maybe used to address areas of weaker ability.

Specifically, *writE science* resources were developed and used across school terms, where these worksheets were applied each week to model and scaffold the skills that students need to gain so they can work towards carrying out an open-ended inquiry. Initially, writE resources present prescribed interventions early in the first term. These worksheets guide students through bounded, scaffolded, and then open-ended activities. In the last three weeks of term, students engage in inquiry projects.

Subsequently, a similar structure has been used at other levels, because the design is adaptable and widely-valued. This application has supported learning for first year university students, master's students, and Year 2 primary students.

The following writeE worksheets illustrate how much detail, examples, help and modelling students may need to learn to be able to observe (generate data), to reflect, to analyse and to organise. The *prescribed* end of the autonomy continuum is as enduringly important for student learning as the *unbounded* end. As indicated in the resource below, it is valuable to provide examples of some of the scaffolding processes from *prescribed* to *open-ended*, so that students will be able to improve and work towards performing a skill.

The left-hand screen grabs are provided as images, not to be read, to give you an overarching sense of the process used. The resources are available at https://www.adelaide.edu.au/rsd/schooling/secondary/resources/.

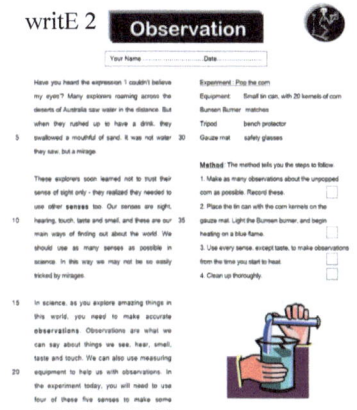

As a part of a set, this *writE science* sheet, writE 2, Observation, provided early in a school term, gives students a highly predictable structured text that makes student note-taking in the 'structured overview' much more effective. The sheet has metacognitive and learning management strategies (e.g., tick boxes) built-in. It explicitly nurtures all six facets in a prescribed way, and focuses on observation skills for generating data.

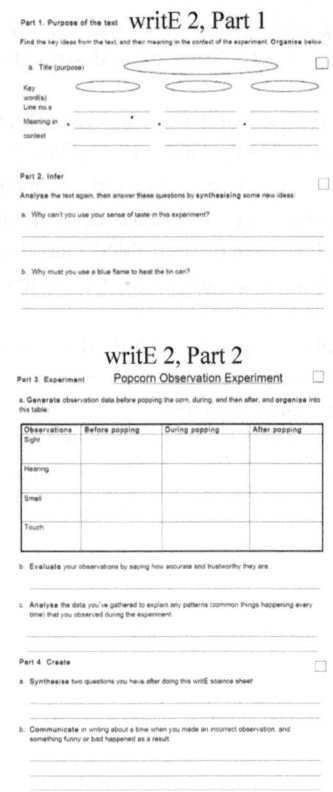

It may be easier for students to find appropriate sources in a web search than to find information in the writE texts. So writE 2, Part 1 requires students to find keywords, the line numbers the words fall on, and the supporting details.

Using that knowledge base, students draw inferences through analysis of text and their previous experience. For this exercise, students' observation skills are nurtured through a structure which organises the observation data they generate.

WritE science helps to differentiate the curriculum by using a structure, and after students demonstrate proficiency, say in note-taking, they may leave out similar sections.

The six facets are needed for the skills of observation (writE 2, Part 2), inference, hypothesising and posing researchable questions in (relating to independent and responding variables). Week after week, these skills are introduced, each drawing on the six MELT facets and increasing autonomy.

Observational skills are facilitated in this writE lab with a focus on four senses. In science labs, teachers often ask ambiguous questions, such as 'what happens to the popcorn when heated?' The question is ambiguous because there is a big difference between observations about 'what happens to popcorn *while* it is being heated?' and 'what happens to popcorn *after* it has been heated?' Requiring students to write down observations of an initial state helps them generate a baseline from which to compare. This process goes beyond mere observing; it is the *generation of data.* Following a focus on observation skills, write Science sheets are used for students to infer, identify independent, responding and controlled variables, hypothesise and pose researchable questions. These resources together develop student sophisticated thinking in a science lab context towards a culminating lab experience; designing their own experiment in writE Science 10.

writE 10

In an open-ended group project (writE 10), students generated their own research questions as a culmination of their saffolded learning. This sheet was the last in the sequence, built on science-specific skills, and revisited all six facets time and again.

The format repeats, enabling the differentiation mentioned above, while autonomy increases over the term. The reading to the left reiterates experimental design considerations.

writE 10, Part 1

The well-structured text above provides students with relevant knowledge on processes which they must use in writE 10, Part 1. Some students still need to take notes, and space is provided for this in the structured overview to the left. Others who have demonstrated proficiency can move directly into addressing the complexities of their experimental design.

writE 10, Part 3

For students who demonstrated competency early in the *writE science* sheets, the MELT Pentagon in writE 10, Part 3 asks them questions that related to each facet. The design encourages students to reflect on their own thinking.

Finally, a story or application of the exercise provided a creative way for students to synthesise their learning.

Perhaps the simplest way to see the embedded differentiation in writE is to view the structure across a school term in resources 1, 2, 3, 4, 7 and 10 at https://www.adelaide.edu.au/rsd/melt/k-12-education#secondary .

By revisiting *writE science* in different terms, participating students engage with numerous ways of generating data. These methods of data generation require them to employ a variety of techniques from descriptive observation to measurement. By connection, students begin to understand that others' information has also been 'generated'. For students, this inquiry raises valuable questions about the trustworthiness of others' information, because they realise all information has a similar epistemological status to their own data.

These ideas of connecting specific tasks and skills to MELT facets happened throughout the term in writE. Later in the school term, students were given a task that facilitated their application of the Year 8 biology skills to the design of their own experiment. In contrast with the popcorn example, there was no procedure given for data generation. Small groups of three students needed to devise their own question, including independent and dependent variables (*embark & clarify*), determine their own method of generating relevant data and apply it to the other four facets of MELT. This scientific strategy remains steeped in the literacy strategy and both have structural similarities of prescribed research to open-ended research. The aim is to facilitate student movement from *emulating* to *improvising* to *innovating*.

3.2.5 Year 7–10 High School Transdisciplinary Projects

In this case, students were provided with workshops that introduced each school's version of MELT, often named the Investigation Framework, for Year 9 or 10. The introduction required students to reveal the sophisticated thinking they used in a highly interactive learning task run during the workshop. Based on their own ways of explaining their thinking, the six facets were introduced and mapped onto their own thinking, so that the students could connect with the wording (Fig. 3.4).

Another approach provides a MELT pentagon which explains the facets in a rudimentary way. Then, students are invited to apply the six facets to a scenario, such as a climactic scene in a widely-viewed movie like *Apollo 13*. Equipped with this group practice of mapping MELT to skills used in the movie, students use the MELT to plan for and reflect on what they will need to learn in order to complete their sustained transdisciplinary projects.

3.2.6 Technical Education

In Technical and Further Education, the Innovative High Achieving Template for Enhancing Maths was developed as a tool for enhancing learning and supporting numeracy skills (Fig. 3.5), with its consoling motto, 'Keep calm, and carry a pentagon'.

What skills did you use to do that?

MELT Facets	Your Analysis
Embark and clarify	Open minded – question – thinking differently
Find and generate	Summarizing- focusing in other idea's
Evaluate and reflect	Evaluating – challenging someone's idea
Organise and manage	Collaborating – work together. Time management. Organising. Multitasking
Analyse and synthesise	Thinking critically- critising advantages. Creative thinking – imagining the test and driving the hours
Communicate and applying	Communication- talking- took turns – listening- quiet – eye contact – open body language. Engaging – acknowledging. Applying someone else's idea.

Fig. 3.4 Skills that students identify that they use to engage in inquiry mapped onto MELT facets. Right column—student inventory of skills used during a learning activity in a workshop. Left column skills are matched with the MELT facets on the left

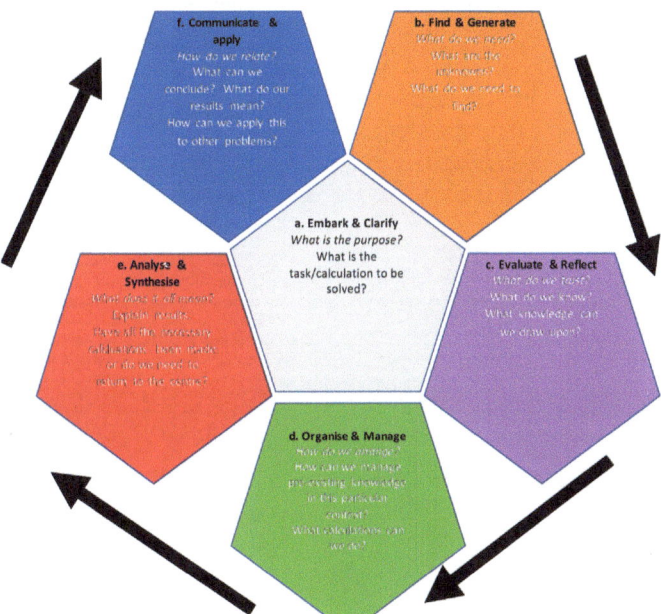

Fig. 3.5 The innovative high achieving template for enhancing maths. https://www.adelaide.edu.au/melt/conferences/short-papers-arranged-by-theme#keep-calm-and-carry-a-pentagon

3.2.7 Undergraduate

Many discipline-specific examples of MELT, especially in terms of assessment, at the undergraduate level are found at: https://www.adelaide.edu.au/rsd/examples/discipline/.

Much of the MELT evaluation studies have been conducted at the undergraduate level. One major study spanned 29 courses in five universities [2] and found that in the timeframe of a semester, explicit skill development makes a substantial difference in student learning. However, it was also found that there was a risk that the thinking skills developed may atrophy. A follow-up series of studies looked at the explicit use of MELT across multiple semesters of a degree in Media [3, 4], Oral Health [5] and Animal Science [6].

An example of MELT use across two semesters is in first year human biology, using the Research Skill Development framework: https://www.adelaide.edu.au/melt/university-learning#discipline

Some aspects of this use follow (Figs. 3.6, 3.7, and 3.8).

The rubric below is available in Word form www.adelaide.edu.au/rsd/examples/discipline/#humanbiology as are dozens of discipline- and task-specific rubrics. Comparing the rubric below with the one above, both use the six facets, but with criteria specific to the task. The above rubric is for a *bounded* activity, and has two levels

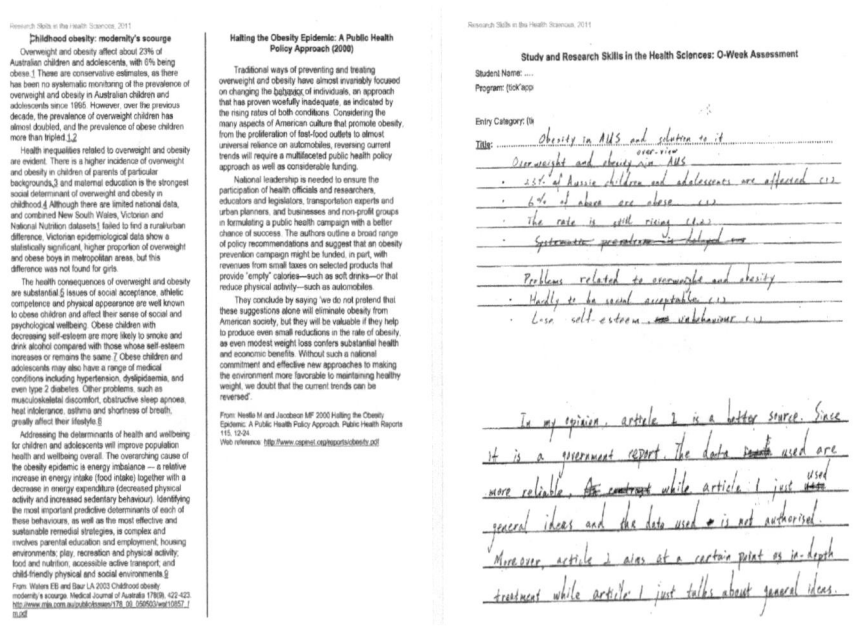

Fig. 3.6 First year human biology diagnostic task: Early in the first semester, students were given two sources (left) from which they were required to take hierarchically structured notes (right). These notes were assessed according to the six facets as used in a task-specific marking rubric (Fig. 3.7).

Research Skills in the Health Sciences, 2011

Marking Criteria for 'O-Week' Research Skills Evaluation

Student Name: _____   Student ID: _____

Marker: _____

Indicators	Level 1	Level 2
The student with research skill ...	Student engages with a closed enquiry and requires a high degree of structure and guidance	Student engages with a closed enquiry and requires some structure and guidance
1. embarks on inquiry and so determines a need for knowledge/understanding	☐ Identifies some *peripheral* or *duplicated* ideas as key	☐ Identifies KEY ideas
2. finds/generates needed *information/data*	☐ Points/notes generated partially relate to the headings under which they are listed ☐ Notes produced are sourced predominantly from 1 text only	☐ Points/notes generated elaborate on the key ideas to which they are linked ☐ Notes produced draw on ideas from both texts
3. critically evaluates *information/data and the process to find/generate*	☐ Identifies indicators of source credibility and reliability but does not fully apply them in evaluating data or process	☐ Identifies several relevant indicators of source credibility and reliability and provides appropriate rationale for usage/inclusion of information
4. organises *information collected or generated*	☐ Has attempted a note-taking framework, but information is organised predominantly as a list of undifferentiated bullet points	☐ Uses a hierarchical note-taking framework that organises related information under the appropriate key headings.
5. analyses and synthesises *new knowledge*	☐ Produces point form notes (information not directly copied or sentence format) but notes separated according to source	☐ Combines and integrates ideas/data from different sources to generate notes
6. applies and communicates *knowledge with understanding and acknowledges cultural, ethical, economic, legal and social issues*	☐ Title is present ☐ Partial and/or incorrect acknowledgement of sources of information	☐ Title relates clearly to the key ideas presented in the notes ☐ Full and correct acknowledgement of sources of all noted information

Fig. 3.7   The rubric structure framed by the six MELT facets was used consistently for assessments throughout two consecutive semesters. The rubric below is specific to a bounded investigation, and Fig 3.9 is for an open-ended investigation, where the facet similarities allowing students to connect the skill set they have been building throughout the year due to the consistent use of MELT facets

Fig. 3.8 Students engaged in an open-ended group project gather life data from tombstones to address their own research question

delineating student autonomy. The rubric below is for an open-ended activity, and so delineates *learning autonomy* into four levels, in the context of the competence expected in first year biology (Fig. 3.9).

Outcomes of this style of use of the RSD have shown substantial benefits for university students in a variety of disciplines and universities [2].

First Year Mechanical Engineering: *Optimising Problem Solving Pentagon*
In 2014, upper-level undergraduate mechanical engineering tutors (University of Adelaide) found that their first year students were not enthusiastic about learning to communicate in a course that focussed on graphic, written and spoken communication skills. These tutors, themselves second to fourth year undergraduate students, took the broad MELT parameters and created the first pentagon version, for direct use with the first year students they sought to support. Since that version of MELT, many of the models are introduced in a pentagon configuration especially when the explicit representation of students' autonomy may detract from the learning priorities (Fig. 3.10).

Further examples are similar in principle to the human biology rubric above, and include second year, third year and honours learning activities. Many details relating to these activities can be found on the RSD website www.rsd.edu.au.

Outcomes of the use of OPS have shown substantial benefits for First Year Engineering students [7].

ANAT SC 1103 Human Biology IB   Semester 2 2010

Marking Criteria for Population Analysis Report

Student Name: ....   Student Number: ....   Marker: ....

← Level of Student Autonomy →

Facet of Inquiry	Level 1 *Students research at the level of a closed inquiry and require a high degree of structure/guidance*	Level 2 *Students research at the level of a closed inquiry and require some structure/guidance*	Level 3 *Students research independently at the level of a closed enquiry*	Level 4 *Students research at the level of an open inquiry, within structured guidelines*
A. Students *embark* on inquiry and so *determine a need* for knowledge/ understanding	❑ Report lacks an explicit statement of Aims (although these may be deduced from report content) and there is no hypothesis	❑ A statement of Aims/hypothesis is present but is either not clearly stated or is inappropriate to the investigation conducted	❑ Report has a clear statement of Aims/hypothesis, that closely reflects exemplars provided in the task guidelines	❑ Aims/hypothesis are clearly stated, focussed and innovative
B. Students *find/generate* needed information/data using appropriate methodology	❑ Source of data is cited (cemetery name/location, ABS, etc) but no details of collection protocols provided, or protocols inadequate ❑ Locates literature relevant to the general topic	❑ Data sampling protocols are adequate but not entirely appropriate in addressing aims/hypothesis ❑ Locates more specific literature on at least one aspect of topic	❑ Data gathered are appropriate to aims/hypothesis ❑ Locates specific literature supporting several aspects of topic	❑ Data from a variety of sources or rigorous data collection ❑ Locates specific literature supporting all aspects of topic
C. Students *critically evaluate* information/data and the process to find/generate it	❑ No awareness of study limitations and biases but an attempt at critical analysis via completion of report self evaluation	❑ Report self evaluation + Limitations or biases of the study design or data collection methods are stated/addressed	❑ Report self evaluation + Limitations and biases of the study design or data collection methods are stated/addressed	❑ Evaluation of the whole study design is rigorous
D. Students *organise* information collected/ generated	❑ Data are gathered but are not presented in a report writing structure Missing _____	❑ Data are incorporated into a report writing structure but there is no clear linkage between sections Poor linkage of _____	❑ Report writing conventions are generally followed with coherent flow Areas for improvement: _____	❑ Report writing conventions are followed completely
E. Students *synthesise*, *analyse* and *apply* new knowledge	❑ There is limited synthesis of study data with existing literature ❑ Results are restated with minimal analysis and discussion	❑ Study data are compared or contrasted with existing literature ❑ Analysis & discussion of data, but misinterpretations/ inappropriate conclusions	❑ Study data are compared and contrasted with existing literature ❑ Analysis & discussion of data is appropriate but omissions evident	❑ Synthesis of study data with that from other studies is rigorous ❑ Analysis & discussion of data is comprehensive
F. Students *communicate* knowledge and the processes used to generate it, with an awareness of ethical, social and cultural issues	❑ Title is present ❑ Sources are cited in the text and LOR, but Harvard referencing style is not applied	❑ Title portrays a general sense of the study content ❑ Sources are cited in the text and LOR using Harvard referencing style but it is inconsistently applied or many minor style errors are present	❑ Title succinctly portrays the full dimensions of the study ❑ Sources are cited in the text and LOR and Harvard referencing is consistently applied although a few minor style errors are present	❑ Title succinctly portrays a study from an "original" perspective ❑ A range of sources is cited in the text and LOR and Harvard referencing is consistently and accurately applied

Fig. 3.9 MELT facets frame the assessment rubric for *open-ended* human biology field research conducted in first year university

Fig. 3.10 The optimising problem solving pentagon. https://www.adelaide.edu.au/melt/ua/media/24/ops_rev5-1.pdf

Optimising Problem Solving (OPS) pentagon
When in doubt, return to the centre

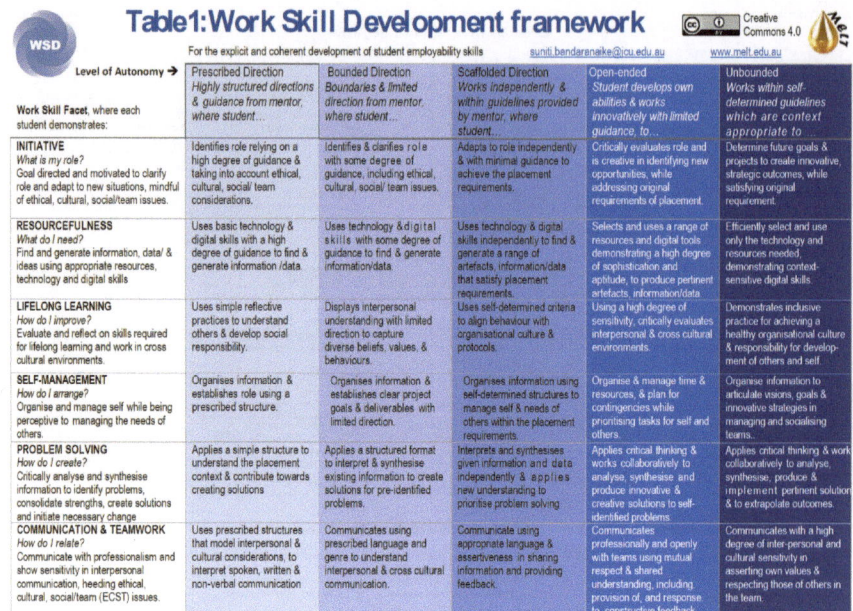

Table 1: Work Skill Development framework — For the explicit and coherent development of student employability skills suniti.bandaranaike@jcu.edu.au www.melt.edu.au					
Level of Autonomy → / **Work Skill Facet, where each student demonstrates:**	**Prescribed Direction** *Highly structured directions & guidance from mentor, where student...*	**Bounded Direction** *Boundaries & limited direction from mentor, where student...*	**Scaffolded Direction** *Works independently & within guidelines provided by mentor, where student...*	**Open-ended** *Student develops own abilities & works innovatively with limited guidance, to...*	**Unbounded** *Works within self-determined guidelines which are context appropriate to*
INITIATIVE — *What is my role?* Goal directed and motivated to clarify role and adapt to new situations, mindful of ethical, cultural, social/team issues.	Identifies role relying on a high degree of guidance & taking into account ethical, cultural, social/ team considerations.	Identifies & clarifies role with some degree of guidance, including ethical, cultural, social/ team issues.	Adapts to role independently & with minimal guidance to achieve the placement requirements.	Critically evaluates role and is creative in identifying new opportunities, while addressing original requirements of placement.	Determine future goals & projects to create innovative, strategic outcomes, while satisfying original requirement.
RESOURCEFULNESS — *What do I need?* Find and generate information, data/ & ideas using appropriate resources, technology and digital skills	Uses basic technology & digital skills with a high degree of guidance to find & generate information /data.	Uses technology & digital skills with some degree of guidance to find & generate information/data.	Uses technology & digital skills independently to find & generate a range of artefacts, information/data that satisfy placement requirements.	Selects and uses a range of resources and digital tools demonstrating a high degree of sophistication and aptitude, to produce pertinent artefacts, information/data.	Efficiently select and use only the technology and resources needed, demonstrating context-sensitive digital skills.
LIFELONG LEARNING — *How do I improve?* Evaluate and reflect on skills required for lifelong learning and work in cross cultural environments.	Uses simple reflective practices to understand others & develop social responsibility.	Displays interpersonal understanding with limited direction to capture diverse beliefs, values, & behaviours.	Uses self-determined criteria to align behaviour with organisational culture & protocols.	Using a high degree of sensitivity, critically evaluates interpersonal & cross cultural environments.	Demonstrates inclusive practice for achieving a healthy organisational culture & responsibility for development of others and self.
SELF-MANAGEMENT — *How do I arrange?* Organise and manage self while being perceptive to managing the needs of others.	Organises information & establishes role using a prescribed structure.	Organises information & establishes clear project goals & deliverables with limited direction.	Organises information using self-determined structures to manage self & needs of others within the placement requirements.	Organise & manage time & resources, & plan for contingencies while prioritising tasks for self and others.	Organise information to articulate visions, goals & innovative strategies in managing and socialising others.
PROBLEM SOLVING — *How do I create?* Critically analyse and synthesise information to identify problems, consolidate strengths, create solutions and initiate necessary change	Applies a simple structure to understand the placement context & contribute towards creating solutions	Applies a structured format to interpret & synthesise existing information to create solutions for pre-identified problems.	Interprets and synthesises given information and data independently & applies new understanding to prioritise problem solving	Applies critical thinking & works collaboratively to analyse, synthesise and produce innovative & creative solutions to self-identified problems	Applies critical thinking & work collaboratively to analyse, synthesise, produce & implement pertinent solution & to extrapolate outcomes.
COMMUNICATION & TEAMWORK — *How do I relate?* Communicate with professionalism and show sensitivity in interpersonal communication, heeding ethical, cultural, social/team (ECST) issues.	Uses prescribed structures that model interpersonal & cultural considerations, to interpret spoken, written & non-verbal communication	Communicates using prescribed language and genre to understand interpersonal & cross cultural communication.	Communicate using appropriate language & assertiveness in sharing information and providing feedback.	Communicates professionally and openly with teams using mutual respect & shared understanding, including provision of, and response to, constructive feedback.	Communicates with a high degree of inter-personal and cultural sensitivity in asserting own values & respecting those of others in the team.

Fig. 3.11 The work skill development (WSD) framework. https://www.adelaide.edu.au/monash.edu/__data/assets/pdf_file/0005/1719401/WorkSkillsDevt-2019.pdf.

3.2.8   Work Integrated Learning

The RSD framework, the first of the MELT has been used to assist in evaluating learning that takes place in industry settings. However, since the terminology of research may not resonate with most employers, Sue Bandaranaike from James Cook University adapted the RSD to develop the Work Skill Development (WSD) framework. Sue Bandaranaike envisioned that the WSD would be used with students and their employers during co-ops, internships, and other work placements—collectively called Work Integrated Learning. WSD use in employment contexts has led to a number of benefits for students, especially their capacity to articulate employability skills [8] (Fig. 3.11).

3.2.9   Course-Based Master's Degree Programmes

MELT has been used in assessment orientations, in ways similar to first year biology examples. Numerous resources, such as examples, tools, descriptions and peer-reviewed journal articles, are available on a master's-specific subsite of the MELT site https://www.adelaide.edu.au/melt-1.dev.openshift.services.adelaide.edu.au/melt/university-learning#masters-by-coursework.

3.2.10 Academic Research: Doctoral, Master's and Early Career Research (ECR)

The Researcher Skill Development framework comprising a learning autonomy continuum delineated into seven levels, the RSD7, was formulated to bring in the unequivocally capital 'R' research into the learning process. The RSD7 can be useful for direct conversations with postgraduate doctoral degree (Ph.D.) students and early career researchers who are thinking about their academic trajectory. It enables conversations or personal reflections on what capacities and skills a researcher can employ, which skills and level of autonomy they seek to develop for the future, and ways to achieve skills and increased autonomy. A study showed substantial benefits arising from the long-term use of the RSD, commencing in Year 1 human biology and then through to the use of the RSD7 in a Ph.D. preparation year (called 'Honours' in Australia) for medical science [9] (Fig. 3.12).

Academic programmes based on sophisticated postgraduate research have also employed MELT successfully. For example, the International Bridging programme at the University of Adelaide asked each doctoral student and their supervisor to assess the student's research proposal using a six-level marking rubric based on the RSD. An article explains the processes used, including the specific marking rubric generated and outcomes on the process [10] (Fig. 3.12).

Fig. 3.12 The researcher skill development (RSD7) framework. https://www.adelaide.edu.au/melt/ua/media/48/rsd7_13nov_15_jm.pdf

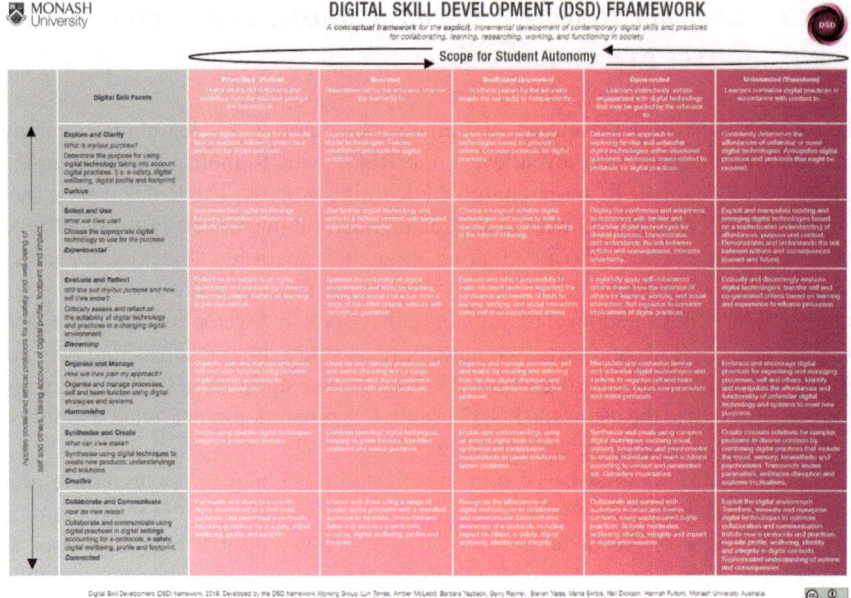

Fig. 3.13 Monash university's digital skill development framework. https://www.monash.edu/__
data/assets/pdf_file/0010/1652437/DSD-document.pdf

3.2.11 Interdisciplinary Studies and Digital Literacy

Two transdisciplinary contexts at the master's level that use MELT-informed rubrics
include addiction studies and climate change [11]. MELT characteristics provided
advantages for facilitating fluid conversations across disciplinary boundaries.

Monash University adapted MELT to be used across disciplines in terms of Digital
Literacy, and produced the Digital Skills Development framework (Fig. 3.13).

3.3 Outside the MELT Parameters

MELT characteristics pertain to a broad range of teaching and learning contexts, from
early childhood to early career research. However, some contexts have requirements
that may fall outside of typical educational settings, but which can still benefit from
applying MELT characteristics. One example, provided by the University of Adelaide, consists of a MELT version that has been tailored towards the Peer Assisted
Study Scheme (PASS, developed at the University of Wollongong). PASS leaders

Fig. 3.14 The pillars in
evaluation (PIE). https://
www.adelaide.edu.au/melt/
ua/media/27/pie_poster_
2017.pdf

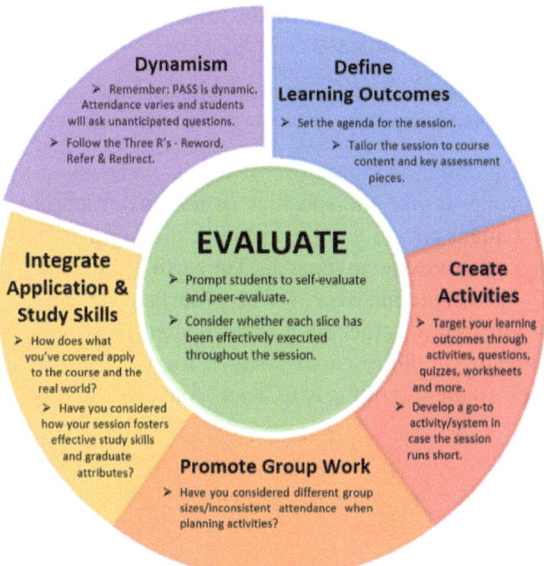

started with MELT, and adapted it to include new parameters which were better-suited to their sessions than the existing ones. These were organised around supporting students dropping in and seeking help for academic purposes and personal development. One beautiful characteristic of their model, the Pillars in Evaluation (PIE), was the facet 'dynamism', emphasising the centrality of fluidity (Fig. 3.14).

3.4 Conclusion: Commonality with Adaptability

Kevin, the graduate who recounted using Silver Fluoride in Cambodia experienced an undergraduate degree that used various versions of MELT—including the Research Skill Development framework and the Clinical Reflection Skills framework—in the first four semesters of the Oral Health degree. In the final year of the degree, students were required to engage in open-ended inquiry. Another graduate of the Oral Health programme said about the development of their sophisticated thinking from the first year that:

You have to research it, you don't get fed stuff anymore. You have to go, research it, sit down, analyse what's important and what's not. So yes, it *slowly did lead up to a better research* in the third year. I think if we started researching in the third year, we wouldn't produce a high-quality piece of work at all (italics added) [5].

This graduate appreciated that, as a student, starting the process of developing sophisticated thinking skills from first year enabled those skills to slowly build up and resulted in better research in the final year because of that ongoing, explicit development. Another graduate of the programme found this scaffolded, incremental, developmental process:

> … encourages all its graduates to have a *mindset of research* on focused learning, lifelong learning and to know that study doesn't stop at the end of the course… (italics added) [9].

The common framing of MELT adapted context-by-context and over time, enables students to take the specifics of any given learning activity, assessment task and individual course and begin to see the big picture by connecting all the parts that may otherwise seem separate. They will perceive, for example, not separate activities, assessments, courses or even separate facet development, but a multifaceted 'mindset of research' or other such sophisticated thinking gems. In a similar vein, a student engaging in the research-oriented fourth year of a Medical Science degree looked back on the use of the MELT and found:

> Since the beginning [of First Year], they have given us assignments based on this criteria. You might not have liked the assignments, but because they have been consistently applying this structure to all of our assignments, we have *come to think that way for science*… [9]

The MELT used as a thinking routine, became for the student a heuristic to think scientifically.

As MELT expands across years of study, disciplines, and learning contexts, students are increasingly likely to be exposed to more than one application of the model. Two of the big advantages of repeat exposure are that (a) it improves student self-assessment and peer assessment, where students become attuned to the standards of the context, and (b) they become better able to work with increasing levels of competency and autonomy in each context.

References

1. Einstein Bubble in Cartoon: Brown, P. (1993). *Managing your time*. Cambridge: Daniels Publishing.
2. Willison, J. W. (2012). When academics integrate research skill development in the curriculum. *Higher Education Research & Development, 31*(6), 905–919.
3. Wilmore, M., & Willison, J. (2016). Graduates' attitudes to research skill development in undergraduate media education. *Asia Pacific Media Educator, 26*(1), 113–128.
4. Ain, C. T., Sabir, F., & Willison, J. (2018). Research skills that men and women developed at university and then used in workplaces. *Studies in Higher Education*, 1–13.
5. Willison, J., et al., (in press). Graduates' affective transfer of research skills and evidence-based practice from university to employment in clinics. *BMC Journal of Medical Education*.
6. Willison, J. W., Al Sarawi, S., Bottema, C., Hazel, S., Henderson, U., Karanicolas, S., Kempster, S., et al. (2014). *Outcomes and uptake of explicit research skill development across degree programs.*Sydney: The Office of Learning and Teaching. https://digital.library.adelaide.edu.au/dspace/bitstream/2440/92390/3/hdl_92390.pdf.
7. Missingham, D., Shah, S., Sabir, F. & Willison, J. (2018). Developing and connecting engineering skills for researching and problem solving. *Journal of University Teaching and Learning Practice, 15*(4).

8. Bandaranaike, S., & Willison, J. (2015). Building capacity for work-readiness: Bridging the cognitive and affective domains. *Asia-Pacific Journal of Cooperative Education, 16*(3), 223–233.

9. Willison, J. & Buisman Pijlman, F. (2016). Ph.D. prepared: Research skill development across the undergraduate years. *International Journal of Researcher Development, 7*(1), 63–83.

10. Velautham, L., & Picard, M. Y. (2009). Collaborating equals: Engaging faculties through teaching-led research. *Journal of Academic Language and Learning*, 3(2), A130-A141.

11. Venning, J., & Buisman-Pijlman, F. (2013). Integrating assessment matrices in feedback loops to promote research skill development in postgraduate research projects. *Assessment & Evaluation in Higher Education, 38*(5), 567–579.

Chapter 4
What Do We Trust?

4.1 Gullible Consumers or Discerning Users?

In the Information Age, students, teachers and learning communities are at risk. The question of what to trust is central throughout formal and informal education. From stranger danger to fake news, from misleading websites to scam journals, questions of trust are tangible. This partially accounts for the frequency of use of the term 'critical thinking' in education. Of course, it is not only students that are challenged by fake information in the Information Age—educators also have to make sense of competing educational perspectives, such as the debate about whether comparative testing facilitates or hinders learning. Information that displays markers of credibility cannot be taken at face value: there are many errors in peer-reviewed journal articles, even in journals with tight quality controls [2].

Another, more buried, aspect of trust concerns the educational perspectives that we hold to. Why is it that some educators lean towards modes of instruction that are highly directed, some towards those that are open-ended, and others somewhere in-between? This too is a question of trust in regard to pedagogies of choice, and determines where we put our concerted efforts, what we can and will achieve as individual teachers, as a whole school community or as a system. But why do some hold a more objectivist rationale, while others are geared towards social constructivist approaches to education? What we trust also determines the types of controversies and arguments we enter into, as well as the resource allocations that affect our students' learning. Building on the core characteristics of MELT as depicted in Chap. 2, and the diversity of its use as shown in Chap. 3, the purpose of this chapter is to use the MELT for reframing the competition between different educational perspectives and dealing with some trust issues. My aim is to show how each perspective may complement the other through the MELT.

J. Willison, *The Models of Engaged Learning and Teaching*,
SpringerBriefs in Education, https://doi.org/10.1007/978-981-15-2683-1_4

In the following section, I present a vignette about Tara, a Year 8 student who engages with a canonical science experiment and declares 'I told you science is stupid 'cause you don't know if you're right.' There are good reasons why Tara declares science to be stupid, and something not to be trusted. This chapter applies the MELT in order to help you ask, 'what do I trust?' It is a challenge to suspend judgement, or at least to give licence to the possibility that educational perspectives other our own may have some merit. We will use the facets of MELT to interpret Tara's story and consider two facets in detail that are crucial to the issue of trust: *evaluate and reflect* and *analyse and synthesise*. We will then use this interpretation to broaden our look across the educational landscape, and turn the question of this chapter to 'why do we distrust other educational perspectives so much?' with consideration for the implications of what we trust and distrust.

The story is called *Shrink*. It describes a situation where I engaged with Tara and her work partner Shannon as a Participant Observer [3] in another teacher's class.

4.2 Shrink

By the time I sit behind Tara and Shannon on the experimental bench that runs along the rear wall, Mrs Stuebalm is already asking the class a recollection question: 'What happens to a gas when we heat it?'

'Expands,' exclaims one of the boys.

Tara calls out, 'Matures.'

I wonder to myself why Tara uses that word.

'This afternoon we are doing another experiment, and I want you to predict what will happen,' says Mrs Stuebalm. 'What do you think will happen if we heat a solid?'

'Expand,' says one of the boys near the front.

'Yes. A very good word,' commends Mrs Stuebalm.

The boy throws his chest out.

'Metal burns and shrinks when you heat it,' adds another boy

Mrs Stuebalm seems to avoid his statement, and immediately asks the students to start writing their predictions in their exercise books.

Mrs Stuebalm refers to a diagram depicting a metal ring. The ring's inside diameter is slightly smaller than the outside diameter of an accompanying metal ball.

She explains, 'What you're trying to do is put the ball through the hoop. You need to be careful, because you could burn yourself. Decide what to heat, the ball or the ring. You have to push it through the ring.'

Tara collects the equipment and sits down next to Shannon at their lab bench. They light the Bunsen, and start heating the ring. Soon, Tara lowers the ball through the hole in the ring, and says, 'We did it!'

She looks very satisfied at their success.

Suddenly, Mrs Stuebalm calls out, 'OK everyone, pack your equipment away. Write down the equipment and tell me what happened to your ball and ring.'

I return to Tara to ask her, 'What was your prediction?'

'Metal would burn and shrink… and that's what happened. It shrinks to let the ball through.'

I'm caught by surprise, but Shannon rescues me.

'No it doesn't. It expands.'

'No, the ring shrinks,' retorts Tara.

'It *expands*.'

'It *shrinks*, because the ring becomes thinner and thinner, until the ball gets through,' explains Tara, getting extremely frustrated with Shannon's thinking.

Shannon is also annoyed with Tara, and retaliates, 'The hole has to get bigger to let the ball through, so the metal must *expand*.'

Tara and Shannon call in Mrs Stuebalm, but the conversation goes round and round in similar circles.

Returning to the front, Mrs Stuebalm asks the class, 'What happens to the solid when it's heated?'

'Expands,' someone calls out.

Mrs Stuebalm nods confirmation.

Shannon whispers to Tara, 'I *told* you.'

Tara sits quietly, looking annoyed. I return to her to try and understand her point, and she continues her explanation: 'I mean it shrinks outwards. Like, the metal inside shrinks towards the outside.'

'You're saying the actual metal bit gets smaller?' I probe.

Tara nods.

'What actually happens is the metal expands and moves out,' I explain.

'I told you!' triumphs Shannon again.

Tara grows even more frustrated, but presses on: 'The outside expands to give the inside room to shrink… see, I said science is stupid, 'cause you don't know if you're right.'

4.3 MELT Analysis of Shrink

In order to consider the question 'what do we trust?' I begin by unpacking *Shrink* through the lens of MELT, considering each facet and focussing especially on *evaluate & reflect* and *analyse & synthesise*. Then, I use *Shrink* as a reflective surface from which to gain perspective on three theories of education.

As with the earlier stories in this book, *Shrink* provides examples of students employing all six facets of the MELT. The scenario in which Tara and Shannon find themselves is a very prescribed and ostensibly simple lab task (see Fig. 4.1). The lab is intended to demonstrate, unequivocally, the canonical idea that 'metals expand when you heat them'. The trouble is that Tara constructs a counter-intuitive interpretation of the results, even though she makes the same observations as Shannon and others in her class.

While this scene is set in a science context, the ramifications are relevant to the ways in which students develop an understanding of core concepts in any subject or discipline. Any student may guffaw, 'I told you this subject is stupid. You don't know

Fig. 4.1 Two students heat a metal ring, so that its expansion allows a metal sphere to pass through it

when you're right'. And the issues for student learning are immense when educators try and fail to help students gain fundamental understanding.

Tara was working hard conceptually to make sense of the practical, and even though the classroom consensus was that 'metals expand when you heat them', Tara would not be persuaded. When I interviewed her one month later about this incident [3], it turned out that she had some good reasons to think metals shrink when heated. She had previously watched her dad soldering, and noted that the soft soldering metal 'shrinks in'. Likewise, throw an empty aluminium can on the fire, she said, and it shrinks. While both these observations are better explained by other concepts (capillary action and chemical change, respectively), I could see that she was basing her current observations on her past knowledge, and that she was striving to make sense of the phenomena. Tara didn't just acquiesce to the classroom consensus or the curriculum; she was willing to challenge both based on what she perceived to be relevent experiences.

In that willingness to challenge the prevailing classroom knowledge, she epitomised the sort of student we are striving to educate—not a gullible consumer of facts, but a discerning user and generator of information. If we are concerned about our students blindly accepting clickbait headlines and 'fake news' by default, we also need to be concerned about how they deal with things that just don't add up for them in our curricula. Tara judged the classroom content, and her verdict was 'science is stupid'. It turned out that she was partly right, in that the experiment, used in science classrooms for a hundred years, is deeply flawed in its design. That the equipment is constructed in such a way as to provide ambiguous data, making it open to interpretation, has been known for some time [3].

All the facets of MELT are present in this story and, as pointed out in Chap. 2, this seems to be typical of even slightly complex learning activities. Even though the location of the lesson on the *continuum of learning autonomy* was *prescribed* in terms of aim, method and final answer, Tara demonstrated something unique in terms of her learning autonomy when engaging with *evaluate & reflect* and *analyse & synthesise*. *Shrink* involved a prescribed practical which was designed to confirm canonical knowledge. However, the complexities and potential sophistication of student engagement with the practical are laid bare when scrutinising it from the perspective of MELT's six facets and autonomy.

Embark & clarify: in the context of the learning topic, the students knew they were doing something concerned with heating solids. The teacher, Mrs Stuebalm, intended for students to learn or confirm that metals expand when heated. Perhaps students other than Tara left the class feeling that they had experienced, constructed and agreed on a scientific 'fact' about metals. And in many ways, Mrs Stuebalm provided a wonderful learning environment, managing the practical risks (naked flames, red-hot metals) and allocating time for an experiment, despite the packed curriculum. As such, the lesson was an ethical and moral endeavour which socialised students into the conventions of science in a way that they could engage with.

However, there is an enduring question for education in this story: how clear was the lesson's purpose to the students? It is difficult for teachers to provide a sense of purpose to students engaging in a series of learning activities across terms and years. If students can't see connections between different activities or develop a sense of purpose, what are the implications for their learning?

Find & generate: the data generated in this practical came from visual observation—primarily, students observed that the ball didn't fit before heating, but did fit immediately after heating. All students 'observed' that the ring's inside diameter grew larger, and Tara and Shannon interpreted this observation in contradictory ways. However, there were no measurements of the ring's actual dimensions, partly due to the dangers of measuring a red-hot ring and the difficulty of obtaining the equipment needed for accurate measurements of the ring's diameter.

Organise & manage: this practical was very quick to complete, and one where you could imagine students having the time to think about its implications. However, for the sake of presenting a succinct story earlier, I didn't mention that the students actually performed several heat-and-expand practicals back-to-back, including one involving liquids, and that these practicals required time to set up, conduct, pack up, clean up and write up. As in *Parachute*, students' ability to develop deep concepts was determined to some extent by their ability to *organise & manage*. This classroom reflected a packed curriculum which, for some students, seemed to impede learning for the sake of coverage.

Communicate & apply: the girls followed a prescribed practical structure to write up their experiment: aim, equipment, results and conclusion. They were not required to draw a diagram, even though a before-and-after diagram would have captured some of the complexity of their thinking. The ongoing communication process was vital to Tara and Shannon's ability to consolidate understandings, and here it was their disagreement that sharpened what they understood to have occurred. Throughout the practical, Tara applied her previous knowledge to the task, making observations based on that knowledge. Her observations and inferences supported the application of her personal theory that *metal shrinks when heated.*

4.3.1 What Did Tara Trust?

Evaluate and reflect: there was little class time to reflect, but as a participant observer in the classroom [3], I had that rare opportunity to interview Tara and Shannonn after the passion of the classroom evaporated. When reflecting on this practical one month later, Tara still thought she was right, and that the classroom science didn't make sense. Her evaluation was quintessential of personal constructivist thinking, and it is rarely so evident as in this account that a student is constructing and weighing up knowledge: 'I said science is stupid'. It may be that the classroom knowledge with which she was presented made her feel stupid, as it didn't fit with her previous experience. Perhaps it unsettled her that self-reflection and attempts to self-correct were of no help 'cause you don't know if you're right.' There is a sense of frustration created by self-doubt. Not only could she be wrong in science, but she would not know that she was wrong, even when she spent time trying to unravel *why* she was wrong.

Analyse & synthesise: everyone, including Tara, inferred that the hole grew larger because of the observation that the ball fell through the hole at the time the ring was heated. However, Tara's theory-laden observation ('it shrinks inwards') led her to strengthen her theory that metals shrink when you heat them. Her classmates considered her to be wrong, even though her analysis made sense in the context of her prior knowledge and her observations. However, instead of being steered into self-correction like the students in *Place Value*, Tara ended up in frustration that you 'never know when you're right'. This is partly because the practical was prescribed in terms of content knowledge, understanding and procedure, with no room for any understanding other than the science canon. Such an approach makes sense insofar as we don't really want students to develop a belief that metals shrink when heated. However, Tara reacted against the correct answer because it conflicted too starkly with the theory she had built for herself.

Tara's analytical thinking was shown in her claim that 'it shrinks outwards. Like, the metal inside shrinks towards the outside.'

'You're saying the actual metal bit gets smaller?' I probed, and Tara nodded.

'The outside expands to give the inside room to shrink.'

Tara's juggling of 'outside' and 'inside' shows that she was considering the width dimension. If one thinks of width, then since metals expand when heated, they would expand in all directions, outwards and inwards. That would make the hole smaller. Because the hole got larger, the opposite must be true: metals shrink to create a bigger hole.

Tara demonstrated ingenious, creative and discerning thinking here to craft her inference based on her observations and prior knowledge. Too bad the class had to pack up, debrief quickly and move onto the next topic. Imagine if the teacher had asked the students to design another experiment to show their ideas, giving them the chance to test some of these or at least think them through. What is a pity is that Tara was thinking in terms of *analysis & synthesis*, but her teacher failed to reward these cognitive skills. For a student engaging in analysis like Tara, science then becomes a 'belief-based subject' in which she should follow the mandates of the teacher, and that such emulation is the only satisfactory way of operating when learning in the classroom. How do those of us with educational responsibilities balance the need to teach students correct content knowledge with the fact that their analytical thinking may sometimes lead them to conclusions which contradict the curriculum? This is another form of the question 'what do we trust?', because what we prioritise indicates what we trust and value.

Within the framework of Bloom's Taxonomy, the knowledge that metals expand when heated is fundamental to students developing an understanding of *why* metals, liquids and gases expand when heated. This is connected to a fundamental theory of matter (called 'kinetic theory') that is often taught in the first year of high school. Without a fundamental understanding of this theory, it is impossible to apply it correctly. Tara could have been guided to consider 'What will happen if you heat the metal ball?' If she had made a prediction consistent with her existing ideas, she would have said that the ball should pass through the ring, since it would shrink when heated. And on observing that the ball did not pass through the ring, she would have been challenged by the phenomena. However, there was insufficient time for this to happen. In terms of the teacher picking up Tara's fundamental error, Mrs Stuebalm did hear Tara's idea. But instead of engaging with her, she proceeded immediately to the front of the room to facilitate a classroom conversation in which the only idea discussed was that metals expand when heated.

Student evaluation, even though hierachically located at the top of Bloom's old taxonomy [4], and second from the top in the new taxonomy [5], acctually is a frequent and recurrent necessity of sophisticated thinking. Evaluation occurs almost always when students are formulating knowledge by internally processing data, information, details or facts. Some of the students in the class depicted in *Shrink* already had the knowledge that metals expand when you heat them, while some may have barely noticed what happened in the practical and just adhered to the teacher's explanation. There may have been some students who had never heard about thermal expansion, but managed to observe the data and construct a phenomena-based knowledge that metals expand when heated. Others may have arrived at the correct conclusion by tuning into the class discourse, relying on the social context, including spoken and written language. Shannon and I were working hard to help Tara comprehend our knowledge, and were using a lot of language and pointing to do so, but Tara's prior knowledge and theories rendered our words senseless to her. She personally constructed and consolidated something that had to make sense to her and, fortunately, she would not acquiesce, because acquiescence would show that she had given up on sophisticated learning in science.

Even in the very simple learning activity of *Shrink*, the empirical substance of which took less than five minutes, learning was very complex and the thinking required to engage with the phenomena of metal and heat was sophisticated. Section 4.5 shows how the multifaceted thinking in *Shrink* renders the perspective of any individual learning theory incomplete, and not to be *fully* trusted to guide the realities of learning and teaching. First, three major theoretical orientations to teaching and learning are summarised and then used to provide perspective on *Shrink*.

4.4   Three Theoretical Orientations to Learning: Objectivism, Social Constructivism and Personal Constructivism

As in most areas of human endeavour, the field of education is characterised by fierce debates about theory. Such debates are necessary: ideally, the theories which provide the best explanation for phenomena become the most popular, allowing disciplines to progress. In the sciences, the 'fittest' theory is the one which is best able to predict phenomena in advance. The scientific enterprise can appear to be frustrated when two long-lived theories, such as relativity and quantum mechanics, fail to connect or to generate compatible predictions [6]. However, some scientists believe that such incompatibility is not a concern, and that each theory is a useful tool of the mind that makes powerful and useful predictions about phenomena that have stacked up over time [7]. For others still, such a clash suggests that both theories may be inadequate, and some deeper theory may be needed.

There are many ways to arrange theoretical orientations in education, and one way of organising them is into objectivism, personal constructivism and social constructivism, three enduringly relevant theoretical perspectives.

Objectivism

Objectivism has as its root a noun, 'the object' [8] which is pre-eminent and must be studied rigorously so that scientists can slowly, progressively and communally reveal an underlying objective reality. A basic tenet of objectivism is that communities of researchers can be confident that, by utilising certain methodological standards, they develop increasingly accurate knowledge about phenomena in the world [9]. A parallel term is 'positivism'. Some say that objectivism was the 'default epistemology' for teaching in Western schools up until the 1980s because it was the only epistemology available traditionally [10].

Objectivism is based on the paradigm that knowledge and truth exist outside the mind of the individual. As such, knowledge and truth are 'objective' not subjective [11]. A teacher or instructional developer who uses a design model based on objectivist thinking analyses the conditions which bear on the instructional system (such as content, the learner and the instructional setting). She uses the analysis to design and prepare the learning environment so that it achieves the intended learning outcomes [12]. Objectivism is typically tied to didactic modes of teaching and learning, like rote learning. It is also tied in with behaviourism [11] and the type of cognitivism that employs a one-to-one correspondence between content and what is learned [13]. Direct Instruction and aspects of national assessment regimes are strongly influenced by objectivism, as is much online learning design and, curiously, the implementation of 'constructive alignment' [14]. 'Curious', because the word 'constructive' was coupled with 'alignment' to connote a constructivist orientation [14]; however, in use, the phrase often boils down to mean 'curriculum that is well structured to achieve its intentions'. The quote above about 'default epistemology' is close to the mark; teachers who haven't consciously thought through their own 'epistemology' or theory of learning will often work from the default setting of objectivism.

Personal Constructivism

Personal constructivism involves internal cognitive processes that build conceptual understanding, based on the foundations of a student's prior knowledge. Learning is a dynamic process, and the way in which learning happens is mediated by internal factors like language, culture and social context. Some personal constructivists see all learning, including research, as a process of trying to ascertain and approximate the nature of objective truth, while others believe that truth itself is internally constructed and does not exist outside of a learner's mind [10, 15, 16].

Social Constructivism

Social constructivism pertains to learning that is co-constructed through interpersonal mechanisms, especially through forms of communication like language. While it is conceivable that a social constructivist may believe in an objectively real world in which we can construct a viable (but never true) understanding, most would hold that the world only is 'real' insofar as individuals or groups of individuals understand it to exist [17, 18].

4.5   Understanding the Three Theories Using the Example of Shrink

Shrink is one example in which a teacher employs Direct Instruction using a pre-scribed practical to engineer understanding of content. All three theories in 4.4 may shed insight into this one practical. One probing question is 'Why did Tara and Shannon make the same observations, but produce such different explanations?' Their analysis was based on different starting points, including their prior knowledge and experience. In science, the dependence of observation on theory has been discussed for a long time [19]; often, we see what we expect to see. However, in this practical, the girls make the same observation that the ball goes through the ring, and both reason that the hole, therefore, got bigger. Then Shannon says, 'The hole has to get bigger to let the ball through, so the metal must *expand*.' Metallic expansion, however, results in a greater volume and surface area of metal. This is the opposite of most experiences with holes, where to expand a hole, we must take something away. If you have a hole in a wall, and a picture plug is too big to go in, you get a bigger drill bit and take away more of the wall. The analysis made by Shannon, Mrs Stuebalm, the rest of the class and me represented a consensus, but it was not in keeping with our general knowledge of holes. That 'metals must expand' may have been for some a recall of the science canon or just a commonly known 'fact'. Others' analyses may have been deductive rather than inductive: 'metals expand when you heat them. We heated the metal ring, so the metal expanded to make the hole bigger.' What type of reasoning was this experiment, designed in the 1900's, designed to elicit? [20, 21].

4.5.1 Objectivist Perspective on *Shrink*

From an objectivist perspective, Shannon appropriately apprehended the intended lesson of *Shrink*, but it is not clear whether the experiment merely confirmed her prior knowledge, or whether she learned something from it. The lesson featured a very clear design pathway intended to lead students to the conclusion that metals expand when heated, a concept that is experienced, talked about between partners, written down in lab books, and discussed in a whole-class debrief. Like Shannon, most students found it easy and efficient to follow the lesson's designed logic.

Concrete and shallow understandings are often the forerunners of children's capacity to think abstractly. It is beneficial to have correct knowledge which concurs with the experiences of the real world, and this provides students with confidence. When they are able to remember facts efficiently, students find it easier to get into a 'learning flow'. Such a state of flow is hard to enter when students have to work things out from first principles each time. Loading up the long-term memory with a host of relevant knowledge and vital concepts is extremely expedient for learning, and this resonates with the children's willingness in *Place Value* to chant together, to rehearse knowledge in order to develop stronger recall. Many students across formal education ask to be told what to learn, so that they know 'what to do'. Some treat this process as mere spoon-feeding, but the desire and capacity to emulate are common in human evolutionary experience, and frequently reflects the way human minds work when learning.

Moreover, certainty in *what* knowledge is needed is something that many students desire and request. Students feel more confident and less afraid of learning when they understand which knowledge they should prioritise. While learning, students don't know where they are going knowledge-wise, and therefore want an educative presence to guide them. Our online and virtual environments provide much opportunity to test and correct student conceptions, such as Tara's, and lead them into the canon of each discipline.

From an objectivist perspective, a one-to-one correspondence between what is taught and what is learned is the ideal, and this is most likely to happen if students attend to the lesson and the teaching material is well structured, with minimal distracting elements. Students acquire a whole lot of 'misconceptions' through play and discovery learning, and these conceptualisations tend to be resilient into adulthood. Furthermore, child-determined play fails to address many concept-based aspects of modern learning, and so time spent 'learning through playing' needs to be strongly facilitated.

4.5.2 Personal Constructivist perspective on *Shrink*

From a personal constructivist perspective, Shannon's prior knowledge was in keeping with the idea promulgated in class, and so her notion was conceptually reinforced, resonating with her understanding. Tara should have experienced a dissonance between her prior knowledge and what happened with the ball and ring as designed by the experiment. That she didn't experience dissonance showed that her prior knowledge was resilient, and that it became the lens through which she made observations. Frequently, prior knowledge is not replaced by canonical knowledge, but students do learn to give the correct answer at times, even if they do not understand or believe the answer. For example, adults tend to maintain childhood conceptions of the phases of the moon, even after correctly answering multiple-choice questionnaires on moon phases when in school [22].

The metal expansion practical was unintentionally designed in a way that allowed for alternative interpretations, depending on students' starting knowledge and experience. Tara's interpretation was sensible and viable, and it would have been educationally useful if she had been given opportunities to further test her concepts using predictions about phenomena and data. Over time, she may have found internal inconsistencies in her understanding, especially if she had encountered dissonant experiences, such as the ball failing to pass through the ring when the ball itself was heated. In that case, she might have formulated new ideas in keeping with the scientific concept that metals expand when heated. However, these would have been based on her old ideas, which are often resilient [23] and may have ended up being the ones she remembered in the long run.

Through its ambiguous design, this practical allowed Tara to reinforce her prior concept. In the future, this practical should be redesigned so that it provides unambiguous data. For example, such a redesign could involve cutting the ring so that it had a gap, which would lead to the hole shrinking when heated, as a result of metal expansion of the ring's width, where not only would the outside diameter increase, but also the inside diameter would decrease [3].

Eliciting student prior knowledge that is in contrast to the canon can prove to be counterproductive. Sometimes, the students are not consciously aware of their understanding until they are asked to articulate their thinking. Once their understanding is brought to the surface of consciousness, students' concepts may become more resilient, or they may be defensive of their own ideas [24]. Even approaches that pay careful attention to conceptual traps, misconceptions and blockages, such as Threshold Concept-based design (see Chap. 5), may not overwrite past knowledge. Research in the area of student development of misconceptions has shifted from perturbing students with 'discrepant events' [25] to encouraging students to place their concepts and newly introduced concepts side-by-side and contrast them [20]. For example, Mrs Stuebalm could ask Tara to predict what would happen to the metal ball when it was heated. If the observation that the ball would not pass through the ring perturbed Tara, but she still did not agree with Mrs Stuebalm's concept, the teacher could ask Tara to compare and contrast 'expand' and 'shrink'.

4.5.3 Social Constructivism on *Shrink*

From a social constructivist perspective, Tara had limited opportunities to construct understandings together with other students, with the teacher or with the whole class. If the social environment had been more clearly thought through, maybe Tara would have come to share the consensus concept, or maybe she would have convinced others of her idea in the short term. Tara showed evidence of previous social interaction— sitting around a campfire with empty aluminium cans placed in it and watching her father weld. This social interaction reinforced her idea that metals shrink when heated. Only well-engineered social environments would have a chance of changing this, and even if Tara were to be exposed to such an environment, there is no guarantee that her new ideas would line up with the science canon. Definitely, there should be more opportunity to deconstruct the experiment and find flaws in it, such as the ambiguous observation data, where 'hole gets bigger' has two opposite, but viable, possible inferences. A preference would be for Tara to design, in partnership with other students, further follow-up experiences in which students made predictions about metal and heating.

Some of the experiences inside the classroom reinforced Tara's idea. When she commented that gases 'mature' when heated, she was not corrected by the teacher. However, as with *Place Value,* the lesson was designed to let students predict and then maybe self-correct through observation, and so Mrs Stuebalm refrained from correcting Tara's early predictions. Therefore, the teacher subtly endorsed the relevance of chemical change for student thinking about observations early in the class. Moreover, another student made a prediction which may well have influenced Tara later: 'Metal burns and shrinks when you heat it'. It may be that this reinforced Tara's existing thinking or it brought back to mind her experiences with aluminium cans around campfires, legitimating the idea that metals shrink.

Future classes would need much more time for negotiation of ideas, preferably with small group presentations on the different major concepts, as well as time for a class debate. If students were encouraged to prepare their points with diagrams and evidence-based arguments, this would emphasise that learning and rational argument are more important than repeating the 'correct' answer. And canonical ideas would probably prevail if this environment were skilfully facilitated by the teacher.

4.5.4 All Three

The issue of whether each student trusts the teacher, their own rational thinking or the social discourse is an important one. Objectivism, personal constructivism and social constructivism each provide a different basis for teachers, parents, administrators and researchers to understand, plan for and determine how to 'measure' learning. From the MELT perspective, all three theoretical perspectives are pertinent and valid. All three can inform the learning that takes place in classrooms [18]. As we saw earlier, theoretical purity is not the default in the sciences, with competing paradigms such as relativity theory and quantum mechanics enduring together.

Instead of being used to direct educators into a narrowed perspective, these three theoretical observations could collectively serve teachers and students to provide understandings of a rich educational experience that is in keeping with the way that learning has taken place over tens of thousands of years. To help make connections between the different perspectives, the next section shows the theory underpinning MELT, and how this theory enables MELT to connect multiple theories.

4.6 Theoretical Underpinning of MELT

Shrink and its analysis are now taken up to consider the theory that underpins MELT. While Chap. 2 outlined the literature that informed MELT, the MELT comprise a conceptual framework for learning and teaching, not a theory. A conceptual framework, such as Bloom's Taxonomy, provides a structure for thinking, and is not by default theoretical. To a large extent, Bloom's Taxonomy, the ANZIIL framework, and the SOLO taxonomy are themselves descriptive. The MELT function at a level that is explicitly connected to practice. However, there is theory underpinning MELT, and aspects of epistemology and theory provide a fundamental understanding of the ways that MELT may provide a conceptual glue between disparate paradigms, theories and practices.

The MELT were designed to provide bridging points between different educational ideas, by addressing multiple theories, and this is enabled in practical terms through the consideration of *learning autonomy*. The MELT always need to become fluid through the warmth of conversation or the heat of the argument. In a similar spirit, Dewey wrote

> It is the business of an intelligent theory of education to ascertain the causes for the conflicts that exist and then, instead of taking one side or the other, to indicate a plan of operations proceeding from a level deeper and more inclusive than is represented by the practices and ideas of the contending parties [26].

These conflicts, before the Second World War, were over similar issues to the issues that are debated today, including the efficacy of inquiry-based learning versus a focus on content acquisition and mastery [26]. In Dewey's terms, no 'intelligent theory' for education has emerged that has provided a 'plan of operations' that includes different perspectives, although classroom teachers themselves frequently take a practical orientation that is 'inclusive' in Dewey's sense. The MELT provide a plan of operations that is inclusive because it spans the gamut of approaches through its elaboration of *learning autonomy*. This section shows how the MELT proceed from a 'level deeper'.

The MELT are theoretically underpinned by conceptual metaphor [27], which allows for the development of an educational perspective from a deeper and more inclusive level. The idea of conceptual metaphor is that for all but the most concrete representations, human conceptual structures resonate with metaphor. From this perspective, 'objectivism' is based on a thing, the object, [6] being real, tangible, comprehensible, so 'objective truth' is where there is a correspondence between the senses and an idea, between what is tangible and what is thought. Objectivism is a complex philosophical position, and within the MELT, it is treated as an extrapolation of a tangible 'object' to a conceptual metaphor [27]. This means that objectivism is treated as a metaphorical perspective or 'reference point' from which to view learning, not as *the* correct way to perceive learning.

Bestowing metaphor status elevates objectivism above being a theoretical perspective that may be proven wrong to an enduring and valuable way of providing insight into engaged learning and teaching. This status also demotes objectivism from being the theory that influences how learning should happen. The net result of this elevation and demotion is to place objectivism on equal footing with constructivism. This equivalent status enables all three theories under discussion to provide valuable perspective on contemporary learning, in keeping with a *continuum of learning autonomy,* which provides equivalent status to teacher-directed learning and student-initiated learning.

Likewise, constructivism is based on the action 'construct'—to build, or the noun 'construct'—what is built. This 'bricks and mortar' idea is related to the internal hidden learning processes in which construction happens. With the different emphases of each, personal constructivism focuses on internal sense-making, whereas social constructivism emphasises the role of language and human interaction in mediating what actually gets to that internal world.

From the formulation of the first MELT, objectivism, personal constructivism and social constructivism were held in tension as helpful and mutually reinforcing metaphors that provide insights into learning and teaching [21]. Rather than treating them as theories that compete, they are more like points of reference [21], places from which to stand and capture insights into educative processes.

4.6.1 Theory on Learner and Teacher Autonomy

Clashes between those with differing theoretical referents and metaphors occur when there is a consideration of how much *learning autonomy* should be provided to specific groups of students. No one argues about *whether* students need to be or become autonomous learners, but they do argue about *when* this should happen. Vygotsky's use of 'zone' in the Zone of Proximal Development (ZPD) [17] connotes a metaphorical region in space, an awareness of a breadth of possibilities. He did not articulate a PPD, a 'Point of Proximal Development', a place where things are 'just right', or a narrow band of performance. In the zone, the part that is closer to the learner is higher in *learning autonomy* as it pertains to the capacity of the learner without support. Further from the learner (towards the outer edge of the zone) is a point beyond her own capacity, but she can successfully demonstrate intended performance at this outer border of competence with support from experienced others. That is, she will demonstrate less *learning autonomy* at this point, and benefit from more guidance, emulating others. With learning that is enabled by such support, a learner increases

Table 4.1 Emphases for objectivism, personal constructivism and social constructivism in terms of the *continuum of learning autonomy*. (The heavier the shading, the more emphasis)

	Prescribed	Bounded	Scaffolded	Open-ended	Unbounded
Objectivism					
Personal constructivism					
Social constructivism					

in her capacity to perform at a more rigorous, sophisticated level. Over time she becomes able to self-direct and self-regulate her learning at this hightened level of competance, *improvising* or even *innovating*, that is with higher *learning autonomy* and with higher competence than before. However, when new concepts are encountered, new skills needed or higher levels of rigour are required, a movement back to the outer edge of the zone, towards lower *learning autonomy*, with guidance from an experienced peer of teacher, is often needed again, with its modelling and structure.

Thus, the ZPD suggests movement from lower to higher *learning autonomy*, from lower levels at the further reaches of the zone to higher levels closer in to the learner's exisitng capacity. Further out, with modelling and guidance, each student learns how to add sophistication and rigour to their learning, and then when the student applies this learning by herself, she works with higher *learning autonomy* in the edge of the zone that is proximal to the student's capacity. For this reason, MELT implies the need for movement from low *learning autonomy* to high, and back [28], like a tidal zone in the complex ecosystem of learning.

From an objectivist perspective, *learning autonomy* should initially be low, providing structured learning environments in which students can acquire a content knowledge base and practice the skills of the discipline. From a social constructivist perspective, autonomy for students should primarily be high, allowing for student ownership and collaborative action. From a personal constructivist position, students are primarily engaging in internal sense-making that emphasises *evaluation, reflection, analysis* and *synthesis*. These facets span from the highly prescribed to the unbounded, with a concentration of effort that is at the scaffolded level, as shown visually in Table 4.1.

4.6.2 Autonomy and Metaphor Together

From the MELT perspective, objectivism, personal constructivism and social constructivism don't need to be competing theoretical perspectives but can be treated as metaphors that mutually support each other. Each brings to the educational table its own set of strengths. An objectivist perspective will emphasise the development of students' knowledge bases and cognitive skill sets, in keeping with *prescribed* and *bounded learning autonomy*. Objectivists, of course, can and do provide more open-ended tasks, but this is typically once the student is demonstrably ready with the required knowledge and skills.

Those who are more closely aligned with personal constructivism will engineer learning environments that enable students to overcome or skirt misconceptions and to develop robust understanding. There may be some rote learning and more open investigation, but there will be much *scaffolded* learning. Social constructivists will maximise motivation, social interaction and student ownership of learning, treating students more as if they are in a learning partnership with teachers, allowing, as often as possible, for *open-ended* and *unbounded* learning autonomy.

Treating each theoretical perspective as a metaphor that connects to parts of the *continuum of learning autonomy* may facilitate a more complementary approach to education than currently exists, as each perspective then merely emphasises a different place on the continuum. Objectivists know that learning the facts and details of a discipline through discovery modes is inefficient, and that it is easy for students to develop misconceptions, and so become frustrated and anxious. Personal constructivists know that didactic teaching and rote learning do not prompt deep understanding, that misconceptions developed while learning are substantial and long-lived, and that frequently there must be structure to learning. And social constructivists see that unless students own their learning and engage in social processes, their motivation to engage and capacity to learn will be diminished. MELT's *continuum of learning autonomy* calls for each perspective to speak to and complement the others, to provide for each student the full experiences of the entire continuum and a shuttling back and forth across it as they traverse the years of education.

4.7 Trusting the MELT?

One aspect of research that we have found so far is that educational gains made over the timeframe of a semester using MELT can be subsequently lost: skills tend to atrophy unless they are explicitly reinforced after they are learned [29]. Facilitating learning is a long-term business, where students' motivation is crucial to what they attend to long-term. Empirically, MELT requires significant timeframes and repeated exposure. Because engagement is a long-term process, MELT must be tested over educationally significant timeframes—a minimum of a term or semester. Neurologically, long-term memory consolidation is thought to take place over years, not days or even terms [30].

Of the many MELT, only three have undergone some long-term evaluation—the RSD [31–33], OPS [34] and the WSD [35, 36]. Conceptual frameworks cannot be effectively evaluated through any one trial because ways of interpreting and implementing a conceptual framework vary markedly. What is needed are sustained use by practitioners and substantial, diverse and numerous evaluations in many contexts.

Chap. 5 strongly endorses educator action research (AR) as a powerful, context-sensitive means of evaluating MELT, especially if the idiosyncratic aspects inherent in AR can be connected together in a common reporting strategy framed by MELT.

In addition to AR, other research methodologies that probe MELT use are needed:

- Fine-grained participant observation studies.
- Studies of change in student performance over educationally significant time-frames (a minimum of one term, but generally multiple terms or semesters). Generally, multiple measures with qualitative and quantitative data triangulation are needed.
- Longitudinal studies that follow cohorts.
- Randomised controlled trials, if ethics and practicalities allow a true randomisation of student and teacher.

Further ideas and support for research into MELT are available on the website [37, 38]. The simple way to proceed to build the knowledge base for all educators is to start with one cycle of action research, with the intention to use MELT to enhance student sophisticated thinking.

4.8 Conclusion: Conversations and Arguments

Although in education we tend to prioritise our theoretical perspectives, education theory has not overwhelmed practice in the same way that, for example, physics practice is dictated by theory. We do need, however, to keep our educational convictions, because the care and drive to teach is one of the beauties of human existence. But conviction does not have to entail self-aggrandisement, the belief that 'I am right' and 'others with different opinions are wrong'. Nietzsche said, 'Conviction is a more dangerous enemy of truth than lies'. A rephrasing may capture the heart of this chapter on 'what do we trust?'—'Conviction *that I am right* is a more dangerous enemy of truth than lies.' Is your conviction about the value of a specific way of educating students? Keep your educational convictions, and act on them consistently. But be a little tentative about how right you may be and how wrong others may be in the light of the complexities of human learning. This requires us to consider what we trust and why, and to hold a little more tentatively our own theoretical or practical philosophies.

The MELT foster argument, but not necessarily in order to bring people to a shared viewpoint. That would be an unrealistic goal, given the range of beliefs, values, ontologies and epistemological perspectives that exist even within any one school system. So MELT are not about 'pulling together' in the same direction, so much as helping people commit to their best teaching while considering expanding along the *continuum of learning autonomy*, to provide each student with a little more shuttling, and connecting a bit more to others' teaching. The sheer volume of disparate teaching efforts is a huge untapped resource in education. Disparate efforts can nullify each other, but they can also co-exist and conceptually connect through a consideration of the MELT's *continuum of learner autonomy* elaborating as they do the *facets* of sophisticated thinking.

References

1. Einstein Bubble in Cartoon: Schwarz, D. (1944, March 12). The Einstein theory of living. *The New York Times Magazine*, pp. 16–17.
2. Nuzzo, R. (2014). Scientific method: Statistical errors. *Nature News, 506*(7487), 150.
3. Willison, J. W. (2000). *Classroom factors affecting student scientific literacy: tales and their interpretation using a metaphoric framework* (Doctoral dissertation, Curtin University, Perth, Australia). Retrieved from https://espace.curtin.edu.au/handle/20.500.11937/268.
4. Bloom, B. S. (1956). *Taxonomy of educational objectives. Vol. 1: Cognitive domain*. New York, NY: McKay.
5. Krathwohl, D. R. (2002). A revision of Bloom's taxonomy: An overview. *Theory into Practice, 41*(4), 212–218.
6. Chapline, G. (2003). Quantum phase transitions and the failure of classical general relativity. *International Journal of Modern Physics A, 18*(21), 3587–3590.
7. Thiemann, T. (2007). Loop quantum gravity: an inside view. In I. Stamatescu & E. Seiler (Eds.), *Approaches to fundamental physics* (pp. 185–263). Berlin, Germany: Springer.
8. Jonassen, D. H. (1991). Objectivism versus constructivism: Do we need a new philosophical paradigm? *Educational Technology Research and Development, 39*(3), 5–14. Sutton, C. (1993).
9. Sutton, C. (1993). Figuring out a scientific understanding. *Journal of Research in Science Teaching, 30*(10), 1215–1227.
10. Roth, W. M., & Roychoudhury, A. (1994). Physics students' epistemologies and views about knowing and learning. *Journal of Research in Science Teaching, 31*(1), 5–30.
11. Wodak, D. (2017). Can objectivists account for subjective reasons. *J. Ethics & Soc. Phil., 12*, 259.
12. Moallem, M. (2001). Applying constructivist and objectivist learning theories in the design of a web-based course: Implications for practice. *Educational Technology & Society, 4*(3), 113–125.
13. Davis, N. T., Jo McCarty, B., Shaw, K. L., & Sidani-Tabbaa, A. (1993). Transitions from objectivism to constructivism in science education. *International Journal of Science Education, 15*(6), 627–636.
14. Biggs, J. (1996). Enhancing teaching through constructive alignment. *Higher Education, 32*(3), 347–364.
15. Kelly, G. A. (1955). The psychology of personal constructs. Vol. 1. A theory of personality. Vol. 2. Clinical diagnosis and psychotherapy. Oxford, England: W. W. Norton.
16. Wadsworth, B. J. (1996). *Piaget's theory of cognitive and affective development: Foundations of constructivism*. White Plains, NY: Longman Publishers USA.
17. Vygotsky, L. S. (1980). *Mind in society: The development of higher psychological processes*. Cambridge, MA: Harvard University Press.
18. Hayes, C. (2018, March). Podiatric medicine and surgery: Situated learning in simulation with social constructivism. Presented at the Health Education England North East Quality Conference, Durham, UK.
19. Schurz, G. (2015). Ostensive learnability as a test criterion for theory-neutral observation concepts. *Journal for General Philosophy of Science, 46*(1), 139–153.
20. Cowie, B., Jones, A., & Otrel-Cass, K. (2011). Re-engaging students in science: Issues of assessment, funds of knowledge and sites for learning. *International Journal of Science and Mathematics Education, 9*(2), 347–366.

21. Willison, J. W., & Taylor, P. C. (2006). Complementary epistemologies of science teaching. In P. J. Aubusson, A. G. Harrison, & S. M. Ritchie (Eds.), *Metaphor and analogy in science education* (pp. 25–36). Dordrecht, Netherlands: Springer.
22. Trumper, R. (2001). A cross-age study of junior high school students' conceptions of basic astronomy concepts. *International Journal of Science Education, 23*(11), 1111–1123.
23. Tytler, R. (2002). Teaching for understanding in science: Constructivist/conceptual change teaching approaches. *Australian Science Teachers Journal, 48*(4), 30–35.
24. Vosniadou, S., Ioannides, C., Dimitrakopoulou, A., & Papademetriou, E. (2001). Designing learning environments to promote conceptual change in science. *Learning and Instruction, 11*(4–5), 381–419.
25. Driver, R. (1989). Students' conceptions and the learning of science. *International Journal of Science Education, 11*(5), 481–490.
26. Dewey, J. (1938/1963). *Experience and education.* New York, NY: Collier MacMillan.
27. Lakoff, G., & Johnson, M. (1999). *Philosophy in the flesh: the Embodied Mind & its Challenge to Western Thought.* New York, NY: Basic Books.
28. Willison, J., Sabir, F., & Thomas, J. (2017). Shifting dimensions of autonomy in students' research and employment. *Higher Education Research & Development, 36*(2), 430–443.
29. Willison, J. (2012). When Academics integrate research skill development in the curriculum. *Higher Education Research and Development, 31*(6), 905–919.
30. Styles, J. (2008). *The fundamentals of brain development: Integrating nature & nurture.* Cambridge, MA: Harvard University Press.
31. Willison, J., & Buisman Pijlman, F. (2016). Ph.D. prepared: Research skill development across the undergraduate years. *International Journal of Researcher Development, 7*(1), 63–83.
32. Wilmore, M., & Willison, J. (2016). Graduates' attitudes to research skill development in undergraduate media education. *Asia Pacific Media Educator, 26*(1), 1–16.
33. Ain, C. T., Sabir, F., & Willison, J. (2018). Research skills that men and women developed at university and then used in workplaces. *Studies in Higher Education*, 1–13.
34. Missingham, D., Shah, S., Sabir, F., & Willison, J. (2018). Student engineers optimising problem solving and research skills. *Journal of University Teaching and Learning Practice, 15*(4).
35. Bandaranaike, S. (2018). From Research Skill Development to Work Skill Development. *Journal of University Teaching & Learning Practice, 15*(4), 7.
36. Bandaranaike, S., & Willison, J. W. (2015). Building capacity for work-readiness: Bridging the cognitive and affective domains. *Asia-Pacific Journal of Cooperative Education, 16*(3), 223–233.
37. Research Skill Development for Curriculum Design and Assessment. (2018). Retrieved from www.rsd.edu.au.
38. Models of Engaged Learning and Teaching (2017). Retrieved from www.melt.edu.au.

Chapter 5
What does it mean?

Analyse & Synthesise

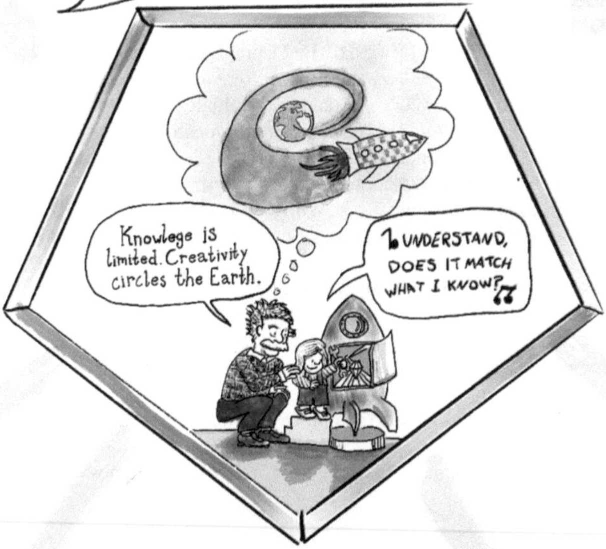

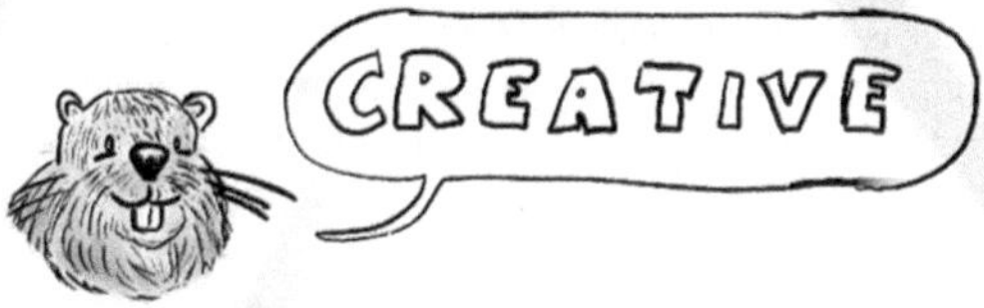

Chapter 5
What Does It Mean?

This chapter focuses on what the MELT mean for education theory and practice. A number of contemporary learning theories (in addition to those discussed in Chap. 4) sit comfortably on the *learning autonomy* continuum of MELT. Some of these sit at the prescribed end, some at the unbounded end and others in the middle. What this means is that the MELT can function as a kind of conceptual glue that holds these often-competing theories in tension: by placing them on the same page, the intention is to open up the conversations between people who hold to each one. Then, based on this complementary view of educational theories, the second half of the chapter considers what MELT means for enhancing learning and improving curricula and pedagogy through teacher action research. This addresses one of the major issues identified in Chap. 1: how to use MELT to engage with educational theory in ways that make practical sense to educators.

5.1 Situating Contemporary Learning Theories/Ideas

This chapter focuses on four educational conceptualisations that have influenced teaching practice in recent years. These conceptualisations entail competing perspectives on teaching and learning and were chosen from a range of possible contenders because they sit fairly well on one end of the *learning autonomy spectrum* or the other and so provide a kind of 'argument from extremes' perspective. However, there are still substantial differences between those conceptualisations at the same end of that spectrum. These four conceptualisations are Meyer and Land's Threshold Concepts [2], Sweller's Cognitive Load Theory [3], Siemens' Connectivism [4] and Schön's reflective practitioner [5]. These three theories and Schön's conceptualisation have influenced education at various levels, from the national curriculum level, to the level of teacher decisions on a minute-by-minute basis. Because of their history and potential future influence on practice, seeing how these theories and ideas may connect together from the perspective of MELT is vital.

© The Author(s) 2020
J. Willison, *The Models of Engaged Learning and Teaching*,
SpringerBriefs in Education, https://doi.org/10.1007/978-981-15-2683-1_5

5.1.1   Threshold Concepts [2]

Threshold Concepts (TCs) are the pivotal learning concepts in each subject or discipline. Within Meyer & Land's theory, these concepts are difficult for students to grasp, making it hard for learners to 'enter through' into discipline-specific ways of seeing the world. For example, in physics, the fundamental concept of inertia (that objects keep moving at their current speed unless a force slows them down or speeds them up) seems counter-intuitive to many. Without understanding the concept of inertia, it is impossible to comprehend Newtonian physics, even if students master the equations associated with motion. TCs are usually difficult or troublesome for learners, and pedagogical structuring is frequently required to enable students to cross the threshold of understanding. The learning involved in crossing this threshold may be frustrating and frightening, and the concept to be learned can seem alien or wrong. In the case of Tara in *Shrink*, the correct explanation of phenomena was opposed to her own interpretation, and so she deemed it 'stupid'. Sometimes, threshold concepts are very difficult to understand in ways that can be operationalised, as in the case of 'controlled variables' in *Parachute*. Sometimes they involve arbitrary conventions represented in absolute ways, such as the left-hand numeral in a two-digit number being worth ten times its face value (as in *Place Value*). Once a TC is crossed over, the concept often seems 'obvious' to the learner, after which it is easy to forget the struggles that such learning requires.

As 'thresholds', such concepts are considered non-optional entry points into learning. Without a fundamental understanding of these concepts, subsequent learning will be superficial and may eventually collapse. In *Shrink*, the idea that metals shrink when heated would ultimately dismay Tara if, for example, she built a brick cooking place with a metal plate measured to fit snugly between the bricks. She 'knows' that the metal plate will 'shrink when heated', leading her to believe that there is plenty of room for the plate. However, in reality, the plate will expand, buckling or breaking the brickwork. If Tara were to become a designer working with metals—a jeweller or architect, for example—her misconceptions could have dangerous and expensive consequences.

Threshold concepts are by definition conceptually demanding, and this demandingness needs to be interpreted according to the age and experience of the learners. For example, an MBA student who has twenty years' industry experience may find it easy to grasp the concept of 'distributed leadership', while MBA students with no professional experience are likely to find the concept much more difficult. Conversely, people with twenty years' experience of top-down leadership may find the concept of distributed leadership an even more difficult threshold to cross. In this latter case, where a TC is counter to a person's experience, educators may need to plan for the student to 'unlearn' an old idea before learning a new one. If there is one thing that is clear from the literature, it is that prior understandings are resilient and difficult to displace [6]. Awareness of TCs helps educators to consider students' existing preconceptions; as such, educators will be less likely to allow students to stumble around with incorrect ideas.

TCs help to explain why students need more than an internet connection if they are to become adept at a particular discipline. Accessing information can lead to a bewildering array of relevant or irrelevant knowledge. Without grasping fundamental threshold concepts, students risk building incorrect models. Threshold concepts require knowledge that is frequently best attained through repeated exposure, experience and educative guidance from an experienced hand.

In terms of MELT, the educative guidance required to cross over thresholds (from a TC perspective) falls within the *prescribed* and *bounded* scope provided by educators. Here, modelling of and guidance into content and concepts are a part of the educational experience that students may need before they are ready for self-initiated discovery. Merely 'telling' a student about a threshold concept does not guarantee that they will internalise it. True understanding of a TC requires more than hard thinking; it may require every facet of MELT, including the application of current ideas and observation of where these fall short. Most commonly, this happens in an environment of low student autonomy, where teachers provide students with a highly prescribed learning environment and the students *emulate*. This can be a good way to help many students move across a threshold, because the teacher will be aware of conceptual sticking points. However, if a lesson pertains to a threshold concept that some have already grasped and others have not, there can be frustration. If the teacher assumes the TC as background knowledge, those who have failed to cross the threshold will feel left behind. Conversely, if the teacher approaches the TC as something that all need to learn, those who have already 'crossed the threshold' will feel bored. In such cases, it can be necessary to provide students who understand the TC with more scope for their learning autonomy.

Once attained, TCs allow students to operate in a whole new way and, in terms of the MELT, the attained concepts enable students to operate with higher autonomy, more ownership and empowerment, until the next TC is encountered. MELT's perspective on autonomy, as unpacked in Chap. 2, suggests a shuttling back and forth between low and high student autonomy. Shuttling back to lower learning autonomy (where teachers *prescribe* and/or students *emulate*) shows a recognition of the need for students to be guided through new TCs.

5.1.2 Cognitive Load Theory [3]

Cognitive Load Theory (CLT) considers the complexities of students retaining, processing and applying information in sophisticated ways. CLT builds on the fairly stable idea that human brains dedicate a lot of storage to long-term memory (LTM), but that there is also 'working memory' (WM) which has very short-term retention of new information and limited storage. WM is a key place where new information is processed, as well as connected and applied to information stored in LTM. Currently, it is thought that humans only deal with around three chunks of new information simultaneously, but that they can also draw simultaneously on their almost unlimited LTM. People learn new information using their senses, and in educational contexts, visual and aural inputs predominate. CLT theorists talk about the 'visual scratchpad', which has a memory of half a second, and an 'auditory loop' which can retain information for up to thirty seconds. If this information is held temporarily in the WM, it can be juggled conceptually.

There are several instances in *Place Value* where the cognitive load is associated with conflicting concepts of value accorded to left–right positions of numbers. This was in evidence when the teacher asked, 'is there any other number in the wrong place?' At first, the whole class called out 'no'. There were multiple loads on their working memory, and together, these may have been partly responsible for the group's unanimous incorrect answer. Some of the cognitive load at that point relates to the question asked early in the lesson: 'Is place value on your right or on your left?' Within a two-digit number, the digit of higher value is on the left (e.g. in '44', the left-hand four is worth forty and the right-hand four is just worth four.). However, in another mathematics convention, numbers of a higher value are placed on the right in a sequence (e.g. 9, 14, 27). This right–left difference for these two conventions is hard enough to grasp when students are learning about double-digit place value for the first time, but much more so when some of these six-year-old students may not be clear about which side is left. In *Place Value*, this set of inherent complications is magnified: students on the *italitali* mat viewed the number sequence back-to-front—it decreased from left to right because it was sequenced from the perspective of the eight students that were facing them. To students on the mat, it appeared as '57, 41, 29, 20, 17, 11, 9, 5'. With this extra extraneous load on each student's WM, the processing time required for the analysis became longer, increasing the risk of inaccuracy, confusion and a feeling of dissonance, all of which may provoke early maths anxiety. In effect, the 'grammar' of mathematics, like any language, is complex and often has internal inconsistencies which can overload WM. Not until students internalise this grammar can the load on WM be lessened when students are dealing with two-digit numbers and be more able to, say, add together two-digit numbers.

We can only process small amounts of new information at a time. These small chunks of information build-up and eventually become part of our personal knowledge base. For short-term memory to be consolidated into LTM requires time, rehearsal and the application of information.

From a CLT perspective, the problem with providing students with higher levels of autonomy is that their STM can become overloaded with new bits of information. Like threshold concepts, CLT provides a rationale for laying down the foundations of a knowledge base, with minimal distracting elements, and slowly building up opportunities to apply that knowledge. From the perspective of these theories, teachers should not consider allowing students to *initiate* until students have demonstrated a mastery of the appropriate content. Shelly struggled in *Parachute* because she did not have the necessary basic concepts in place, such as the formula to calculate the area of a square. Kevin's success in *Silver Fluoride* is based on the fundamental knowledge and skill base that he developed during his degree, and which therefore prepared him to *initiate* sophisticated learning.

CLT and TCs are contemporary learning theories/ideas that provide an impetus for learning to be engineered, prioritising the lower end of the *learning autonomy* continuum, where teachers *prescribe* and students *emulate*. But another current and influential theory sits at the opposite end of the *continuum of learner autonomy*: connectivism.

5.1.3 Connectivism [4]

Connectivism focuses on knowledge being distributed in networks and doesn't differentiate information from knowledge and learning. Siemens positions 'knowledge' as a construct that can exist externally to a learner. Information and knowledge can be stored, for example, in papyrus scrolls and hand-copied books. Information and communications technology (ICT) merely speeds up the sharing of information, as did the move from hand-copied books to the printing press. However, modern ICT is qualitatively different from those technologies in that it also enables the consumer to be a producer, and to dynamically engage with and change the knowledge representation. This can involve commenting on, modifying or creating from scratch, uploading a video, or compiling mash-ups.

For Siemens, the goal is to put knowledge into action at the point of application. Where the student lacks that knowledge, he or she draws on 'the ability to plug into sources to meet the requirements…' (p. 2). When knowledge is not the Bloom's Taxonomy-like foundation for learning, but rather the learner's purpose is, control shifts from a knowledge-giving teacher towards the learner. For connectivism, then, knowledge is not a fundamental basis for learning. Rather, knowledge is an enabler, a part of the learning process, not the beginning of it. Importantly, knowledge is, in effect, injected when needed in the learning process, and this resonates with non-sequential, multifaceted learning. For example, if a student is exploring how to code a robot so that it is able to walk up a ramp, the student may go online, or visit other knowledgeable students in the class to get that information at the time the student perceives she needs it. This could be contrasted with the teacher providing all class members with the information that he thinks necessary about uphill coding, at the time he thinks it needed. For MELT facets, connectivism elucidates that 'clarify… the knowledge required' does not necessarily come first. It may be well into an investigative process before further knowledge needed is factored in by the learner themselves.

According to Siemens, the acceleration of knowledge production means that current knowledge becomes quickly outdated. This short life expectancy of knowledge currency means that learning 'can now be off-loaded to, or supported by, technology', contrary to theories like CLT and TC, which focus on students' cognitive processes. 'Know-how and know-what are being supplemented with know-where (the understanding of where to find knowledge needed)' (p. 2). From the MELT perspective, finding others' information requires all six *facets*, especially clarification of what is sought, methodologies to find and the interrogation of sources and their content. Siemens further probes the times when knowledge is not the starting point for learning: 'How do learning theories address moments where performance is needed in the absence of complete understanding?' (p. 5). In contemporary, interconnected learning, there is certainly a case for high levels of autonomy and prioritisation of just-in-time searches to get the job done, and this is true for professionals as well as students.

Connectivism emphasises interconnectedness among students, as well as between students and educators: 'We can no longer personally experience and acquire learning that we need to act. We derive our competence from forming connections of each other' (p. 2). Students connect to each other in a way that is analogous to the connection between partners in a business. The bigger the business, the less each partner knows about the whole enterprise, and the more specialised individual knowledge becomes. The company's knowledge resides in the interconnectedness, in the networks between different employees, as well as between employees and knowledge-containing devices. At face value, for MELT, this interconnectedness enables foregrounding the self-determination of what to know, how to know it, and therefore of higher student autonomy. However, given the nuances of autonomy, such enabling really depends on the nature of the relationships, and if there are any educative relationships.

5.1.4   Schön's Reflective Practitioner [5]

Schön's reflective practitioner (RP) is an individual who has powerful internal resources at hand. Such an individual has the capacity to reflect on the action and teach themselves as they go. In some ways, the RP concept is the opposite of connectivism, in that the RP's knowledge is not distributed and networked, but localised. In other ways, RP and connectivism are complementary, as they both defer towards higher learner autonomy (*improvise* and *innovate*). Within both perspectives, student ownership of the learning is paramount.

Schön's two big self-teaching tools are reflection-in-action and reflection-on-action. Reflection-in-action occurs when a professional faces indeterminate decisions, that is, ones in which the correct choice is not obvious. According to Schön, practitioners make off-the-cuff decisions using a detailed and nuanced 'know-how'. Whereas some may write off this idea as a 'gut-feeling', Schön considers such decisions to reflect an underlying expertise and experience. Like practitioners, students can learn to take what they know and act. However, Schön's second reflective component is a vital component of this process.

The second component of Schön's model loosely corresponds to the standard view of reflection: reflection-on-action. This type of reflection is carried out after the effect, sometimes spontaneously (in musing or conversation) and other times systematically (in diarising or recording). Reflection-in-action can be done with specific frames of reference in mind, such as conceptual frameworks or theoretical positions (like CLT or connectivism). The 'reflective surface' one uses for reflection determines the character of those reflections. For Schön however, the emphasis of reflection-on-action is the process of looking back at the indeterminate decisions made through reflection-in-action, and teaching oneself. Therefore, knowledge external to the learner and others' theories are secondary to internal decision-making, which provides a powerful impetus to learn. Together, reflection-in-action and reflection-on-action make Schön's Reflective Practitioner a strong learner, able to improve and exercise high levels of autonomy.

At the same time, not only do each of the theories sit on the *continuum of learning autonomy*, but also in their various foci, each requires all six MELT facets. For example, given MELT's ancestry of Information Literacy standards, with their focus on 'information-seeking behaviour', the *know-where* of connectivism requires all six facets of MELT. As stated earlier, know-where is 'the understanding of where to find knowledge needed', and in many ways it is a form of 'know-how'. One reason for this is that 'where' is not merely the location of a source, but the level of relevance and trustworthiness possessed by that source. Likewise, 'know-where' cannot connote something effective for learning if it were to merely 'relocate' knowledge from one position to another. In addition, there must be analysis and synthesis that are dependent on effective organisation and that are enabled by, and lead to, effective communication. Across all these MELT facets, the students increasingly need to clarify their purpose, especially if the beginning is vague due to a lack of clarity from teacher instructions or due to the student's own lack of specificity. As noted in Chap. 2, in the flood of irrelevant information, clarity is power [7]. Einstein makes the same point on the Chap. 3 title page: 'Out of clutter bring simplicity' [8]. To paraphrase and synthesise both quotes 'powerful thinking results from learning how to clarify the clutter' and this requires all six facets of the MELT. Thus, the MELT perspective about sophisticated thinking is not so much 'higher order thinking' in keeping with Bloom's taxonomy, but *multifaceted thinking*.

5.1.5 Corporately Destructive or Mutually Informative?

The four contemporary learning theories/concepts described above are current and appealing. However, when we compare them to each other, we find apparent tensions between them in terms of what teachers ought to emphasise. These tensions may be relieved by placing each of the theories/concepts along MELT's continuum of student autonomy. Doing this provides an understanding which propels shuttling back and forth along the continuum. There are various challenges to each of the four perspectives above, especially from each other. While two are especially information and knowledge focused, one of these—Cognitive Load Theory—posits that learning occurs in an individual's brain, while the other—Connectivism—defines learning as something distributed outside any one's brain. The other two perspectives emphasise deep understanding, and where Threshold Concepts prioritise the inculcation of foundational concepts by teachers, the Reflective Practitioner employs and values learners' existing resources and intuitions. Conceptualisations that have overlap, then, occupy 'competitive spaces', and so, in effect entice adherents to warn about the perceived dangers or deficits of neighbouring competitors. For example, one article focused on the new learning taking place due to learning technologies is titled 'A Pedagogical Paradigm Shift from Vygotskyian Social Constructivism to … Siemens' Digital Connectivism [6]. This 'shift', demanding a conceptual migration, shows that the notion of 'academic tribes' [9] is alive and promotes competition fostered in defending or expanding the conceptual territory. This competition is useful if one theory or concept may be or become the best, most parsimonious, most informative for teaching and learning. Given the histories of education and most disciplines, this is not likely, and so treating theory as literal, as really describing the learning condition, rather than as more metaphoric in nature, diminishes the potential for mutually reinforced connections that the MELT continuum of learning autonomy makes possible. This competitive stance of territorial tribes has until now merely diminished and made disparate the energies in education for teaching, learning and research and reduced their effectiveness but could, in the near future, have more sinister effects.

5.1.5.1 Epistemologies of Machine Learning

Disparate and competing views make the educational enterprise, broadly speaking, more vulnerable to vested interests and to the emerging new world order, especially that mediated by machines. Just like the theorists above, humans currently working on AI and Machine learning are working on issues of epistemology. Machine Learning has to be on some learning platform or other and the issue of epistemology—or how learning happens—dynamically influences and is influenced by that platform. At a mechanical level, some AI learning platforms mimic the neuronal architecture of the human brain, whereas some are altogether different. Quantum computers will probably be a key component of AI operating systems, with possibilities including 'a neural network encoded in the quantum properties of light' [10]. We do not know what will comprise the intelligence of AI because the possibilities are numerous and broad, and include hybrid versions of old-style analogue computing and quantum computing [10]. With the advances in quantum computing, it is difficult to know which platforms or combinations will learn best in which situations. At a processing level, it has been known for a long time that machine epistemology is or can be very different from human epistemology [11] but because the structure of AI will not be clear for a long time, the epistemologies of AI will likewise remain unknowable until they fully emerge or diverge. Well before we can understand Machine Learning, however, we will have to understand Machine Pedagogy, for this will dynamically influence student learning in classrooms.

5.1.5.2 Epistemologies of Machine Teaching

AI used in schooling and university education for teaching will face unresolved epistemological questions just like all AI, but it is the pedagogy that machine teachers use on children that will impact first. We do know that the machines that teach children will need to choose or have chosen for them learning theories that are suited to humans not machines. An AI teacher may derive human learning theories itself, discarding all those that have preceded, and use a grounded theory approach [12] because, after all, machines will use data from children learning, in order to formulate their theories of teaching. Alternatively, specific learning theories may be prioritised by some programmers of teaching machines. For example, one study found that 'The results suggest that integration of certain *behavioral theories* as features in machine learning systems provides the best predictions' [13] (italics added). Currently, students learning to read, as mediated by reading robots, seem to develop a strong bond to the robot, and these robots could be programmed with a Social Constructivist epistemology where correction may be secondary to connection. A robot programmed with a behaviourist orientation, however, would favour correction over connection in order to provide correct stimuli leading to correct response. This raises an issue that has been endemic in education. What works 'best' depends on what you value in your measurements, with objectivists valuing, and so measuring, quite different things from constructivists.

In the short to medium term, it is likely that parameters for learning theories that machine teaching will operate by will be set by human programmers. This may result in some incredibly consistent teaching, and maybe even highly creative, varied machine teaching, engaging students within the boundaries set. But it also risks escalating paradigm wars to new levels, with AI programed to follow parameters that prioritise one end of the learning continuum or the other. It could result in unequivocal understandings about the superiority of a theory in a specific set of circumstances, and/or in vested interests competing for the commercialisation of their AI/paradigm package.

AI could, of course, be programmed with parameters that allow for and encourage the full spectrum of theories, interpreted along the MELT continuum of learning autonomy. The window of opportunity for educators to play a role in determining such parameters is closing and with late 2023 being when the earth is predicted to hit 8 billion people alive at the same time, that provides 2020–2023 to make decisions that will impact on the education of the next billion human brains. The main readership of this book, teachers of young children to supervisors of PhD students, have a little time to inject a deeper sense of humanity into the debate about Machine Teaching. Maybe parents and other citizens would like to think too about the ramifications of narrow or competing sets of learning paradigms for machine teachers. In addition, all of us have to wonder if we want a future where human teachers are increasingly irrelevant, and where maybe there is little point of human learners when machine learners get all the jobs.

Each perspective in 5.1.1–5.1.4 provides a currently useful consideration for engaged learning and teaching, each can be challenged by the other theories, and each can be placed on the *extent of autonomy* continuum. Placing them in such a way allows each theory to be held tentatively, without considering any of the four to represent 'the truth'. Weighing together different educational theories helps us to understand how they can inform and improve engaged learning and teaching. When we bring in Machine Learning and Teaching, the stakes about differences in learning theories become much higher, mission critical. While we have human teachers, or maybe to keep teachers human, what are the insights that learning theories can provide to improving student learning, when viewed in a complementary way through the MELT?

5.2 MELT for Curriculum Design and Improvement

Using MELT to connect different learning theories has practical implications for student learning. Firstly, curricula need to have strong conceptual underpinnings. Such underpinnings help teachers to facilitate student acquisition of a contemporary knowledge base and investigate areas of interest in ways that develop sophisticated thinking and rigour. Secondly, curricula themselves need to improve and adapt over time in order to enhance learning and teaching. By using MELT, educators can hold a variety of perspectives, such as Direct Instruction and discovery learning, so that instead of conflicting, the perspectives can work in unison to inform curricula and their improvement. MELT reduces educators' obligation to choose one perspective or theory only, and increases their capacity or willingness to hold several in productive tension. Such multiply-informed curricula, taken together as a set over time, may better scaffold the development of sophisticated thinking when compared to a set of curricula informed by a narrow range of strategies. This is only true if a way of connecting, like MELT, enables teachers to conceptually unite a variety of perspectives so there is a legitimate coherence between them.

Which curricula are best able to provide learning that spans learner autonomy, that enables the acquiring *and* construction of students' own knowledge, and the simultaneous development of the skills associated with sophisticated thinking? The answer is not in the curricula, which vary enormously, but in how teachers bring a particular curriculum to life, improving it over time through planning, implementation and revision. Ongoing improvement of this kind is here called 'action research', and maybe an imperative to keep teaching human.

5.2.1 Teacher Action Research

Action research entails teachers intentionally enhancing the conditions for learning through spirals of action and improvement, in contexts for which they have direct responsibility. Much published educational research comes under this definition of AR, although such research is frequently labelled as something else. The component of the definition from which some people distance themselves is 'have direct responsibility for'. One reason for this distancing is that a phenomenon for which the researchers have teaching responsibility entails a 'subjective' engagement rather than 'detached' observation. In terms of standards of objective research, subjectivity is a no-no, but in terms of curriculum improvement, there are many advantages to teacher-as-researcher, with a strong interest in attaining positive outcomes for student learning.

The rich contextualisations and nuanced descriptions possible in AR mean that it is more likely than many other research approaches to overcome the theory–practice gap [14]. Through AR, practitioners can put theory into action in ways that make sense to them. This means that the typical problem of 'translation' of research findings is minimised, because during AR, theory is translated as the research is carried out. AR should be communicated not as an account that is generalisable to any context, but with rich descriptions to enable another practitioner to read, understand and transfer thoughtfully to their own context [15].

Action research is a useful methodology for consolidating existing good practice, because teachers often try one intervention at a time, leaving most of their practice untouched. Some people with a strong policy orientation push for wholesale change [16] rather than gradual change, but this can be highly problematic for at least five reasons. One is that the useful, evolved and adapted knowledge of a community can be thrown out in big change, whereas AR is good for consolidating practices which already work. Second is that teachers can struggle to understand initiatives imposed by others, whereas AR typically *is* the teacher's own initiative. Third, policies are easy to implement badly, but difficult to implement as intended. Fourth, different teachers have differing personalities and theories of education, both of which influence implementation, and so large-scale changes can lead to highly variable outcomes. Even providing a uniform curriculum to multiple classes through forced training and tight invigilation of teachers is very difficult, and can be counterproductive. Fifth, those who pilot initiatives and show good outcomes are often those who chose to be involved. There is a risk that the second generation of implementers demonstrates less effective outcomes than the self-selecting first generation [17]. Action research inevitably leads to change, as suggested by 'action'. However, such change can simply mean the maintenance or tweaking of existing approaches. This may be one of the features that make AR effective.

AR accounts for who and what teachers actually are: people with emotions and a teaching sense. They may slide between professional pride and care to apathy, disengagement and anxiety. A motivational starting point in AR is for teachers to resolve an issue that is important to them. This builds on their existing thinking and can lead some to find a way out of anxiety or apathy. A disengaged teacher is an ineffective teacher, and telling teachers what to do more forcefully or with greater incentives does not always work. Giving a disengaged teacher some real say in design or implementation can be a way to improve their teaching. Degrees of rigour and sophistication need to be added to spirals of AR, which should increasingly reference quality criteria [18] and enact these over time.

The ownership of a teacher AR is empowering and has the potential to produce something akin to the Hawthorne Effect [19]. The Hawthorne Effect was named after a phenomenon found during research on productivity in the Hawthorne factory. Researchers found that while an increase in luminosity increased productivity, decreasing luminosity had the same effect. They surmised that the workers responded to the actions or presence of researchers, and this response was independent of lighting levels—rather, it was cued by the *change* in levels.

The researchers' findings from the Hawthorne factory may have been unhelpful for employers seeking to fine-tune lighting levels. However, the findings are very useful for those who want to improve student learning in contexts for which they have direct responsibility. Students can tune into the fact that the teacher is doing research and trying to find ways of improving their learning. Teachers will be interested in the outcomes of their designed intervention. But the Hawthorne Effect suggests that any intervention, if perceived as an innovation or change in practice, alerts students to something, and this alert enhances their learning. As a result of the Hawthorn Effect, one of AR's apparent weaknesses—subjectivity due to teachers' ownership of the research outcomes—becomes a strength, actually enhancing student learning while AR is happening.

Typical AR spirals proceed as follows: identify problem or issue, plan an intervention, implement, evaluate and identify further cycles. But there are three problems with this standard sequential model. First, such a sequential representation does not capture the messy, recursive nature of actual research (including AR). Second, this simplified sequence does not reflect forms of research other than AR, and so it reduces the status of AR to something less than research, something you do if you can't do anything else. Third, and most importantly, this neat and linear conceptualisation minimises the effectiveness of AR because it does not incorporate the conceptual prompts or challenges needed to increase rigour and sophistication of research and action over time. This compromises possibilities for improvement.

MELT's six facets can help teachers inform their action research into curriculum improvement so that they add rigour and sophistication over time. From the perspective of MELT's six facets, AR involves messy, recursive processes where teachers: identify the issue, problem or aspect that could be improved; imagine improvements, find information that could be relevant, find relevant data or generate new data; evaluate information for pertinence and for trustworthiness; organise information so that trends can be seen for detailed analysis and manage the time, resources and strategies used; look at information from other classes, the web or the literature and synthesise new, creative answers to address the issue; and weave communication and application of knowledge throughout the whole process.

MELT, if used as a scaffolding for the structure of teachers' AR conceptualisations, has a four-fold imperative. Firstly, teachers can use MELT to inform curriculum design. Over time, this could include making connections to others' curricula, for the purposes of planning and implementation. Secondly, when used as a thinking routine, MELT help teachers to facilitate student awareness of their own thinking. Third, teachers may use MELT skills to inform their own action research in terms of planning, implementing and evaluating improvements in teaching, learning and the curriculum. This enables an intersection of the learning, teaching and research through MELT-informed conversations between educators and researchers. Finally, by using MELT to inform their AR, teachers can come to understand how their individual research may better connect to others' curriculum research.

5.2.2   Conjoined Action Research: From the Transferability of Individual Studies to Generalisability When Using an a Priori Framework

Educational researchers tend to value generalisable results over idiosyncratic research such as AR. This may be a big problem for education, because applying generalisable results to the classroom is difficult [20]. While the notion of generalisable results is highly appealing, methodologies designed to achieve such results have serious limitations. And while individual AR is not generalisable, each instance of AR has the capacity for transferability. Moreover, if there are ways that different instances of AR can 'speak together', then they may have elements in common that can, over time, reveal trends that are generalisable.

In education, generalisability is sought through Randomised Controlled Trials (RCTs). Whereas RCTs are often thought of as a gold-standard of research with humans, in education they have many limitations because they possess low ecological validity, are highly resourced and typically conducted in educationally insignificant timeframes [16]. Here, 'low ecological validity' means that the research is far away from 'business as usual' due to: the presence of researchers not normally on-site; extra resources or funding that may not be available once the research is complete; contact with parents and students to achieve informed consent; randomisation into treatment and control groups, creating artificial groups of students or temporarily isolating individuals; and a quick injection of treatment or control group learning protocols [18].

RCT designs in education typically take place over educationally insignificant timeframes, such as a lesson, a day or a week. The real-time measures immediately after an intervention are a time-bound way of capturing student learning. RCTs provide an immediate extrinsic motivation to engage in short-term learning and testing in ways that cannot easily be mirrored in the standard classroom. Informed consent normally means that some students and parents opt-out, and so the cohort is less representative than if all students were involved, and those who opt-out maybe those for whom the intervention is less suited. Moreover, even with those who consent, true randomisation is very difficult to achieve, due to timetable constraints.

A Nature journal survey of authors who published scientific, generalisable research found study results were not replicated in follow-up studies conducted by other researchers (70% non-replication) [21] or even by the same team (50% non-replication) [21]. This means that generalisability in experimental work such as RCTs 'depends' on the research team. RCTs within the complexities of education are unlikely to be more rigorous than medical RCTs which involve, say, an intervention requiring regular doses of a medicine.

Action research, on the other hand, is conducted in naturalistic ways and timeframes. Here, 'naturalistic' means 'implemented in classrooms with levels of resourcing that are not added to by researchers' budgets and collaborations'. The associated timeframes tend to be educationally significant: a term, a year or multiple years. Extended timeframes provide far more credence for classroom practice, because

Table 5.1 Comparison between RCTs and AR

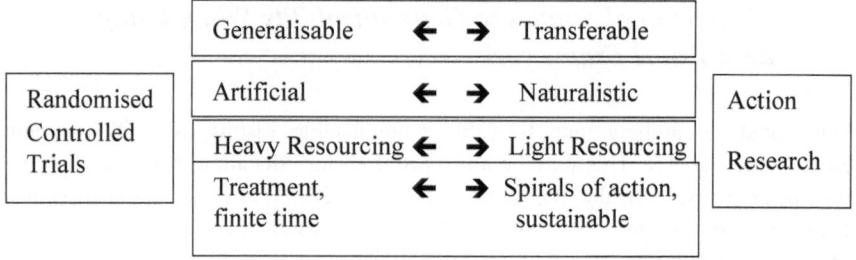

teachers engaging in AR have to deal with aspects that RCT approaches see as 'confounding', such as student motivation to engage long-term in the learning.

Action research is powerful because it is fitted to the specific context in which it is enacted, by the teachers who have responsibility and ownership of the learning environment. This leads to ownership of the research, a strong interest in positive outcomes and steering towards the best student learning possible. While the researcher has a vested interest to confirm that their own approach works in AR (compromising the study's objectivity and generalisability), this is also AR's strength, for positive learning outcomes provide an endorsement of teacher professional judgement. The teacher's ownership of the research speaks to the heart of their educational prowess, a self-validation but not a generalisation to other contexts. Table 5.1 shows the features of AR when compared to RCTs.

Analysis of multiple MELT-informed AR studies could inform not only individual implementers, but assist a move from transferable to generalisable research. A systematic review of studies about research-based learning found that the amount of guidance provided by teachers to students was reported in an ad hoc manner. The review's authors, therefore, recommended that an a priori framework be used for reporting [22]. MELT's continuum of *learning autonomy* provides a cross-studies language to describe 'amount of guidance', and along with the six facets, it provides an a priori framework that is both adaptable and readily useable for reporting. Meta-analyses of AR, if MELT facets and autonomy are used to connect multiple studies together, may show that these studies have some generalisable findings. MELT as an a priori framework for analysis and reporting can connect the reportable outcomes of otherwise non-generalisable AR, providing a trend over many studies.

Action research can begin with low rigour and sophistication, but as AR continues, it should demonstrate increases in rigour as part of the learning inherent in research as a process. A practical way of adding rigour is ensuring that AR researchers use and report on all of the facets of MELT. Increases in rigour can be assisted by reflection-in-action, and simultaneously by adding to personal, idiosyncratic approaches, those informed by the literature. As an example of increase in rigour, Table 5.2 considers pertinent questions, facet by facet, early and later in AR cycles of actions. With MELT to inform ways to lift rigour of AR processes, and to enable connections between different AR studies, this gives AR the means to improve student learning in ways

Table 5.2 Questions and issues for each facet and level of learning autonomy in relation to commencing AR and maturing AR

	Early cycle of AR	Later cycles of AR
Embark & clarify What is my purpose?	What is my biggest problem?	What problems are endemic across the years of Science, English, etc.?
Find & generate What do I need?	Do I have an idea worth trying? Who can I ask?	What approaches are in the literature? What data can I collect that is relevant?
Evaluate & reflect What do I trust?	Is this the best option to try?	How trustworthy is the data I collected?
Organise & manage How do we arrange?	How will I implement this?	How do I sustain this with other teachers?
Analyse & synthesise What does it mean?	How much did this approach improve student learning?	How much did this change colleagues' understanding about student learning?
Communicate & apply How do we relate?	How do I tell my students?	How do I tell parents, school staff or an educational conference?
Extent of Autonomy	How much guidance do they need?	Can students negotiate their own preferred autonomy?

that RCTs cannot. Multiple AR studies of contexts with educationally significant timeframes may over time show the benefits of interventions more effectively than RCTs. If MELT is used to frame the reporting, multiple AR studies conducted in naturalistic settings with little extra resourcing may coalesce on the same findings over time. This would then provide rich descriptions for reported AR outcomes so that they can be transferred to the classroom, and synthesis that shows trends across many AR studies and contexts.

5.3 Conclusion: Multifaceted Use with the Same Overarching Purpose

MELT helps teachers to interpret educational theories by plotting them along the *learning autonomy* continuum. This allows them to connect to and use theories as part of their teaching repertoire. For example, if a teacher needed to choose between CLT or Connectivism to inform a contemporary curriculum design, each theory implies a very different design with correspondingly different learning opportunities for students. However, connecting these theories through MELT using the *continuum of learning autonomy* to inform when and how to use each theory can help teachers design a curriculum which is more holistic and helpful for engaged learning.

Action research, informed by one or several theoretical frameworks, can be conceptualised and reported in the terms of MELT. This use of MELT will not only allow different educational theories and perspectives to speak to each other, but will provide the scope to draw together separate instances of teacher AR and report the analysis of the trends and synthesis as more generalisable results.

The huge untapped resource in education is the sum of separate efforts. These efforts sometimes exist in conflict, but can reinforce each other through a consideration of the continuum of *learning autonomy* and the six facets of MELT. The conceptual power of MELT, as a consolidation of 100 years of educational research and 100,000 years of human learning, is the connections it forges. This power can enable students to connect all their learning together across the years and teachers to connect to each others' curricula and to educational theory as they engage in systematic AR informed by MELT, in order to develop student sophisticated thinking.

References

1. Einstein Bubble in Cartoon: Nilsson, J. (2010). Albert Einstein: "Imagination Is More Important Than Knowledge". *The Saturday Evening Post.* Accessed from https://www.saturdayeveningpost.com/2010/03/imagination-important-knowledge/.
2. Meyer, J. H., & Land, R. (2005). Threshold concepts and troublesome knowledge (2): Epistemological considerations and a conceptual framework for teaching and learning. *Higher Education, 49*(3), 373–388.
3. Sweller, J. (2011). Cognitive load theory. In *Psychology of learning and motivation* (Vol. 55, pp. 37–76). Academic Press.
4. Siemens, G. (2005). Connectivism: learning as network-creation. *ASTD Learning News, 10*(1), 1–28.
5. Schön, D. A. (1987). *Educating the reflective practitioner.* San Francisco: Jossey Bass.
6. Kivunja, C. (2014). Do you want your students to be job-ready with 21st century skills? change pedagogies: A pedagogical paradigm shift from Vygotskyian social constructivism to critical thinking, problem solving and Siemens' digital connectivism. *International Journal of Higher Education, 3*(3), 81–91.
7. Moallem, M. (2001). Applying constructivist and objectivist learning theories in the design of a web-based course: Implications for practice. *Educational Technology & Society, 4*(3), 113–125.
8. Harari, Y. N. (2018). 21 Lessons for the 21st Century. Random House
9. Trowler, P. R. (2001). *Academic tribes and territories.* McGraw-Hill Education (UK).
10. Carleo, G., Cirac, I., Cranmer, K., Daudet, L., Schuld, M., Tishby, N., ... & Zdeborová, L. (2019). Machine learning and the physical sciences. arXiv preprint arXiv:1903.10563.
11. Resch, M., & Kaminski, A. (2019). The epistemic importance of technology in computer simulation and machine learning. *Minds and Machines, 29*(1), 9–17.
12. Salam, A. F., Nahar, S., & Pervez, S. (2019). integrating machine learning and grounded theory research. *Proceedings of the Twenty-fifth Americas Conference on Information Systems,* Cancun, vol. 1, p. 1–5.
13. Plonsky, O., Apel, R., Ert, E., Tennenholtz, M., Bourgin, D., Peterson, J. C., ... & Cavanagh, J. F. (2019). Predicting human decisions with behavioral theories and machine learning. arXiv preprint arXiv:1904.06866.
14. Ulvik, M., Riese, H., & Roness, D. (2018). Action research–connecting practice and theory. *Educational Action Research, 26*(2), 273–287.

15. Lincoln, Y. S., & Guba, E. G. (2016). The constructivist Credo: Yvonna S. Lincoln Egon G. Guba. In *The Constructivist Credo* (pp. 25). Routledge.
16. Jacobs, A. M., & Weaver, R. K. (2015). When policies undo themselves: Self-undermining feedback as a source of policy change. *Governance, 28*(4), 441–457.
17. Joshua, J. (2017). Economic policies of economic growth and development. In *China's Economic Growth: Towards Sustainable Economic Development and Social Justice* (pp. 45–80). Palgrave Macmillan, London.
18. Tracy, S. J., & Hinrichs, M. M. (2017). Big tent criteria for qualitative quality. *The International Encyclopedia of Communication Research Methods*, 1–10.
19. Sedgwick, P., & Greenwood, N. (2015). Understanding the Hawthorne effect. *British Medical Journal, 351*, h4672.
20. De Coninck, K., Valcke, M., Ophalvens, I., & Vanderlinde, R. (2019). Bridging the theory-practice gap in teacher education: The design and construction of simulation-based learning environments. In *Kohärenz in der Lehrerbildung* (pp. 263–280). Springer VS, Wiesbaden.
21. Baker, M. (2016). Is there a reproducibility crisis? A Nature survey lifts the lid on how researchers view the crisis rocking science and what they think will help. *Nature, 533*(7604), 452–455.
22. Lazonder, A., & Harmsen, R. (2016). Meta-analysis of inquiry-based learning: Effects of guidance. *Review of Educational Research, 86*(3), 681–718.

Chapter 6:
How do we relate?

Chapter 6
How Do We Relate?

This chapter shows that what is needed in formal and informal education is not only the connections between theories and practice that have been called for so far in the book but also something that enables people to genuinely relate to each other and disparate ideas. This chapter asks, 'How do we relate?' Like other MELT questions, we can ask this question in relation to the small scale: within a class, or a small group investigation before lunch. Or we can ask it in relation to a larger scale: how do we relate learning from one lesson to the next, from one subject, one term, one year, one stage of education to the next? Ultimately, the question becomes 'how do we relate our thinking about teaching and learning to that of other educators?' The MELT provide a conceptualisation that represents these different progressions, people and perspectives, and that facilitates connected relationships.

This chapter focuses on the problems associated with the relationships between humans, as well as relationships between humans and the planet. It looks at why things have proceeded in a direction that was, to a large extent, inevitable in terms of how human solutions to problems, including technology, caused problems that were sometimes larger than the ones originally solved. However, now that we have a more comprehensive view of the planet than ever before, the chapter moves on to consider whether our future is, or may become, a little less inevitable. As noted in Chap. 5, part of the solution to entrenched or emerging problems is rethinking what theory does for education, and taking a complementary rather than a competing perspective of theory. This will enable more unified efforts towards providing learning environments that develop thinkers who can solve humanity's and Earth's problems.

First in this chapter is a story about cosmonauts and astronauts uniting in space during the middle of the Cold War. This story is a reminder that connections between clashing perspectives can be worthwhile and powerful, and that such connections can be made against all odds. The story provides context for how we might relate to

© The Author(s) 2020
J. Willison, *The Models of Engaged Learning and Teaching*,
SpringerBriefs in Education, https://doi.org/10.1007/978-981-15-2683-1_6

those with perspectives on important aspects of life (including education) which are the polar opposite of our own.

Energies of teachers and researchers need to unite around shared, adaptable and culturally sensitive models for education that graduate students who have the research mindedness to solve the many entrenched problems, and new problems that will plague us from 2040, in a way that does not create additional problems. How do we enable the next billion brains born to become primarily constructive people who desire to build up society, the environment and each other? Student sophisticated thinking requires faciliation by professional teachers who are not forced into 'best practice' by others, but have the discernment to be constructive. For students and teachers alike, to be constructive is not to be persuasive or building-oriented, but nurturing and full of care.

6.1 Soyuz and Apollo: A Story About a Cold War Meeting in Orbit

The communist USSR and the capitalist USA arguably represented the twentieth century's most polarised, long-term adversarial positions. But in the Smithsonian Air and Space Museum in Washington DC, there is an amazing configuration: a re-enactment of a moment from 1975, when, in the middle of the Cold War, the USSR and USA cooperated at the highest, most sensitive and most complex levels (Fig. 6.1).

In the museum is a thirty metre contraption comprising a USSR-era Soyuz craft docked with a US Apollo module. Despite the two nations' adversarial politics and their appearance of extreme competition, especially in space, both realised that the competition would kill them. To begin to unite on earth, they chose a symbolic act of

Fig. 6.1 Apollo and Soyuz coupled in the air and space Museum, Washington, D.C.

uniting in space. This act is not famous, but the docking of the craft may have been the beginning of the end of the Cold War.

The Apollo–Soyuz Test Project required both groups, years in advance of 1975, to share top-secret information on guidance systems, space hardware and software [2]. The two ships were very different. For example, their entry hatch sizes were incompatible, so a three-metre 'docking unit' needed to be engineered for the event. The Soyuz normally operated on pure oxygen at 1/3 atmosphere, whereas the US craft used air at 1 atmosphere [2]; the Americans would have blown up the Russians had they docked and connected their triple-pressure atmosphere. The two teams had to share trajectories, launch times, positional information and operational information. Then the astronauts needed to engage with the cosmonauts socially—they couldn't dock and sit in separate capsules! They had to be willing to communicate with those who had not only a different mother tongue, but a very different ideology. The language barrier was perceived to be one of the biggest obstacles, and so the Americans learned Russian before launch and spoke it in when docked, while the Russians learned and spoke English [2]. The crews ate a meal together, shared memorabilia, signed international certificates and hoped, as their respective presidents watched via a live telecast (alongside millions of their citizens), that 'our joint work in space serves for the benefit of all countries and peoples on the earth' [2].

I am writing this on the eve of the fiftieth anniversary of the first moonwalk, but that event further escalated the Cold War, whereas the Soyuz–Apollo Project helped to defrost it. The threat of mutual annihilation provoked by the nuclear and space race was a sufficient stimulus to prompt changes in the way that the USSR and the USA related to each other. However, to actually change political and public sentiment is a highly charged affair, and the Soyuz–Apollo docking was a kind of circuit breaker that allowed high-voltage differences to leak out over time. It is salient that the event which generated more tension (the moon-landing) is famous, while the one that began a genuine connection between warring parties (the Apollo–Soyuz docking) is almost forgotten. As a species, we tend to prefer winning over cooperating, and this is food-for-thought for anyone involved in educational disconnections.

Current global deterioration, one would think, should be enough to prompt a similar response. However, we no longer feel the sense of urgency that came with the possibility that one button-push could launch the world into a nuclear winter. Our concerns about nuclear annihilation come and go with the news headlines. Our biggest current earth-wide issues, however, arguably involve a slow decline of the planet's ecosystem, causing habitat destruction that is induced especially by overpopulation pressures and the increasing prosperity sought by billions. This slower-speed issue is hard to resolve without concerted, unified and sustained agreement by many governments. While the overarching problem of the Cold War was evident, it is difficult to even identify the problems facing Earth in 2020, and there are now many more parties involved than the two main governments of the Cold War. Maybe a big circuit breaker equivalent to the Soyuz–Apollo is needed, or maybe a very different kind of solution. We do know that we need a billion problem solvers whose solutions anticipate and avoid subsequent problems.

6.2 Inevitable Earth

Humans for 100,000 years have been outstanding problem solvers. However, as noted in Chap. 1, many of the solutions we have found have resulted in further problems which are more difficult to solve than the ones we started with. So our skill at solving problems was, in part, a function of the sheer number of problems we caused, including the Cold War.

This capacity to solve problems while inadvertently causing more problems does not mean that humans are wicked and greedy in a way that separates them from the rest of nature. Rather, the process was inevitable. A species so well-equipped for sophisticated thinking, with a body that could work in a way that corresponded to that thinking, was powerfully adaptive to its environment for 100,000 years. Then *Homo sapiens* began to adapt the environment to suit it, tens of thousands of years ago [3]. At first, such adaptations of the environment were small: the intentional use of fire to manage foliage and grazing [3], or the collection of grass seeds in the fertile crescent in order to sow it in a specific well-watered location [4].

In addition to achieving what was intended, some problems' solutions produced unanticipated effects. Planting grass seeds allowed small populations to remain in one place for longer, reducing the need to travel and more predictable food supplies made it possible to establish larger family groups [5]. The consequent rise in population afforded our ancestors more protection from predators and from competing bands of humans [6]. Escalation of agricultural technology ensued, providing a competitive advantage over humans who did not plant seeds [6]. Technology compounded, with success growing on the back of technological success [7]. But no-one anticipated the inevitable problems associated with such success. How could *Homo sapiens* have anticipated such problems?

Until around 50,000 years ago, nothing humans did compared to the environmental change wrought by beavers (as noted in Chap. 1). Had beavers been equipped with learning brains and grasping thumbs, they might have caused far more environmental degradation than they did, at a rate that would have put humans in the shade. However, super-specialisation locked them into a niche that was hard to break out of, and even in 20 million more years, beaver descendants may still be dam engineers. In contrast, humans were generalists, able to run (slowly), climb (poorly), fight (weakly), build (badly) and learn adaptively. While we may be slower than cheetahs, weaker than gorillas and less architecturally intuitive than termites, our learning capacity means that we will almost inevitably land a human on Mars. That is, unless the compounding problems associated with our compounding solutions catch up with us first! An Earth human population which crashes to several million, say, following an environmental cataclysm, is going to have problems visiting the neighbours on the other side of the stream [8], let alone getting off the planet.

Given human brain capability and our anatomy, it was inevitable that human capacity got us to this point of compounding problems. An interesting example of inevitable, compounding problems cropped up yesterday when I attended a public presentation on quantum computing [9]. The presenter argued that quantum computers would be able to hack existing digital security protocols within the next five years. The only remedy he presented for this was the adoption of new quantum computer-generated security systems. Such a state of affairs is reminiscent of a self-fulfilling prophecy, where the need for a technology is, in part, created by the existence of the technology. A reflection on the inevitability of this process may take some of the pressure off us. We are a self-incriminating species, and it can help to pause and understand that we are, or were, part of the biosphere—not especially weird or holy or special.

However, understanding the inevitability of a deteriorating Earth is not an excuse to say, 'that's fine'. We can now see the entirety of the planet and understand our place in it. Indeed, since Yuri Gagarin's journey in 1961, we have been able to see the whole Earth from space [10]. With our information gathering and sharing, we can now perceive in great detail our impact on the planet, and with that knowledge we have a chance to make global deterioration a little less inevitable. More than ever, we are able to see the extreme social stratification and isolation, environmental degradation and species extinction, as well as escalations in our capacity to annihilate. But our ability to observe these problems does not guarantee that we will do anything effective about them.

6.3 Evitable Earth

If we continue in our very intelligent ways of solving problems, then maybe the fate of the Earth is sealed: inevitable species extinction and a human population crash. For a model of the scale of crash possible, the Mayan civilisation was thought to comprise between 15 and 30 million people at its peak, and the population crashed to thousands in several decades [11]. If a crash of similar severity were to hit the planet in 2023, this would mean that the population of 8 billion humans would be reduced to a few million. Such a crash has happened more than once in large and small human populations, and it could happen on a global scale [11].

There are not currently any palatable solutions to mitigate the problems we face with a large human population. In 1979 or earlier, China elected to minimise its population growth through the one-child policy. This resulted in the 'prioritisation' of boys over girls, with estimates of girls 'missing' in China varying from 20 million to 160 million [12]. As is common, our solutions often have perverse and unpredictable consequences that cause more problems.

Therefore, it is no longer enough for us to merely solve problems. We need minds that can genuinely anticipate problems that will result from solutions and mitigate these or, even better, look for solutions that 'first do no harm'. If our education systems can produce critical thinkers capable of creative solutions that anticipate subsequent problems, our earth's immediate future may be a little less inevitable. In order to lead us to a trajectory where planetary destruction is not assured, these thinkers will need to be primarily 'constructive', rather than self-serving or ideology-based, and have had a mind-expanding education. With a connected education informed by MELT, they could prompt a less fated, more evitable earth trajectory with room for hope.

6.4 Retheorising Theory in Education, from 'Competition' to 'Complement'

From a MELT perspective, each passionately held theory and approach can help the community to build a little towards a mind-expanding education. Let educators and parents with different perspectives talk and, if they are 'poles apart', at least perceive the ground between the poles. For example, a big focus on content acquisition may have some great advantages in terms of discovery learning, if students have learned some key and pertinent ideas. Likewise, discovery learning might be a great motivator towards learning content. In *Parachute* (Chap. 1), Shelly knew about independent and dependent variables, and she may have acquired these concepts in a *prescribed* context. She applied these tricky concepts in a personal instance of discovery learning that was *open-ended*. Although she faced many difficulties, she applied the concepts of experimental research effectively, and conducted research that demonstrated sophisticated thinking in a science context.

From the MELT perspective, there is no philosophical law against jumping from facilitating *prescribed* to *open-ended* learning nor from *unbounded* to *bounded* learning. But teachers implementing a curriculum need to have discernment and power to implement their well-reasoned judgements about what is best for each situation. MELT can enhance the capacity for discernment, because as an analytical tool, it is functional, addressing the practical questions, 'what do these students need?' and 'how much guidance?'

If we treat theories, by definition, as competitive, then we may continue to have a problem. Given the complexities of learning and teaching, educational theories may need to complement each other more and fight less. Seeing theories and perspectives as more metaphorical and less literal might help educators to at least acknowledge theories that are a pole away from their own perspective.

In Chap. 1, I proposed the enterprise of educating human brains so that they have the capacity to solve problems without causing unanticipated additional problems. This educational wiring would involve brains that have a substantial content knowledge base of fundamental concepts. It would also involve brains that take risks, delve into issues and problems, and are highly discerning. While learning content and learning through delving can be presented in mutually exclusive ways, in MELT they belong to the same *continuum of learning autonomy*. Rather than conflicting with each other, they are complementary.

Tara's resilient understanding of content in *Stupid* was contrary to the scientific canon. She showed that we cannot merely say, 'Give students lifelong learning skills. All the information they need is available, so they just need to know how to access it.' This is a very tenuous position to hold, no matter how often it is said. If we don't understand ideas, we won't even know what we are holding, and we certainly won't be able to readily synthesise multiple ideas.

This next billion humans born from 2023–2030 may be the make-or-break generation. They will inherit all the problems of the planet, including those which have been made, inevitably, by the 100 billion other brains that came before them. They will enter formal education from 2024 onwards, and most of those billion will complete their compulsory education around 2050. The problems we face and will face are still improperly identified,hidden or not yet created, and the solutions are out of our present-brained generation's league. Overall, MELT is an opportunity to put into the hands of the billion the sophisticated thinking tools that they will need. These are the tools of the inquiring ape, because these tools of sophisticated thinking are the best we have. But now we need to connect disparate efforts and contexts so that we can 'rachet up' our sophisticated thinking to enable us to solve problems with solutions that first do no harm.

6.5 Conclusion: It's Only When We Relate to Divergent Practices, Concepts and Places in Education that We Will Solve Our Educational Problems

As a species, we named ourselves the 'wise man'. For an animal that destroyed its own environment through desertification, salinification, heavy-metal contamination and warfare, the word 'wise' seems a little off-the-mark. Beavers, with their smooth brains and genetically stored behaviours for dam construction radically altered their environments, but at such a pace that ecosystems were able to evolve along with the change. Our learning brain seems to learn too fast for ecosystems to catch up, but not fast enough to enable us to craft solutions that don't make things worse. We are both too smart and not wise enough.

If we haven't been particularly '*sapiens*', could we become a little more aware? Business, military, health and even educational interests compel us on the same inevitable trajectory as that taken by the 100 billion brains born so far. Maybe MELT can help broker a broad union of educational perspectives so that, working in mutually reinforcing ways, our species may become *sapiens* in action as well as in name, following a new, more evitable earth trajectory.

References

1. Einstein Bubble in Cartoon: Paraphrased from Einstein, A. (1934). On the method of theoretical physics. *Philosophy of Science, 1*(2), 163–169.
2. Redmond, C. (2004, July 19). *The flight of Apollo-Soyuz*. Retrieved from https://history.nasa. gov/apollo/apsoyhist.html.
3. Harari, Y. N. (2014). *Sapiens: A brief history of humankind*. New York, NY: Harper.
4. Diamond, J. (1997). Location, location, location: The first farmers. *Science, 278*(5341), 1243–1244.
5. Holliday, R. (2005). Evolution of human longevity, population pressure and the origins of warfare. *Biogerontology, 6*(5), 363–368.
6. Armelagos, G. J., Goodman, A. H., & Jacobs, K. H. (1991). The origins of agriculture: Population growth during a period of declining health. *Population and Environment, 13*(1), 9–22.
7. Van Schaik, C. P., Pradhan, G. R., & Tennie, C. (2019). Teaching and curiosity: Sequential drivers of cumulative cultural evolution in the hominin lineage. *Behavioral Ecology and Sociobiology, 73*(1), 2.
8. Diamond, J. (2013). *The world until yesterday: What can we learn from traditional societies?*. London, England: Penguin.
9. Sparkes, B (2019). *Quantum of promise*. Public presentation. University of Adelaide, Adelaide, Australia.
10. Faure, G., & Mensing, T. M. (2007). *Introduction to planetary science*. Dordrecht, Netherlands: Springer.
11. Diamond, J. (2005). *Collapse: How societies choose to fail or succeed*. London, England: Penguin.
12. Kennedy, J. J., & Shi, Y. (2019). *Lost and found: The missing girls in rural China*. New York, NY: Oxford University Press.

Chapter 7

How much guidance?

Learning Autonomy

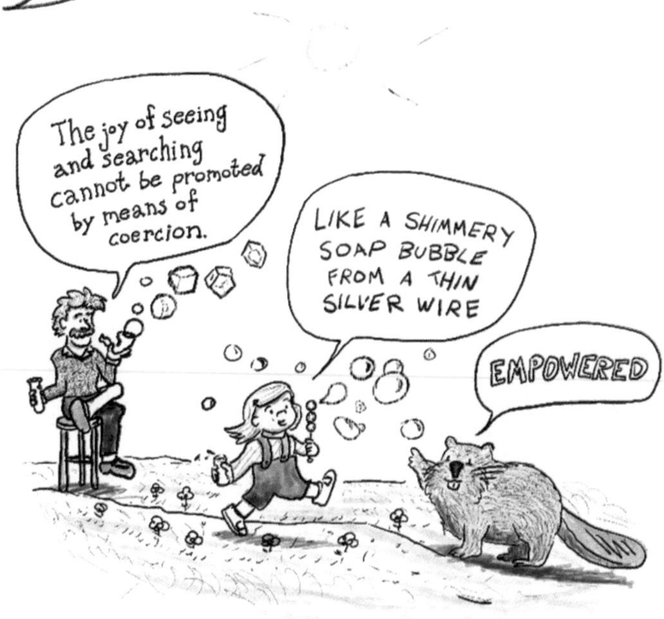

Chapter 7
How Much Guidance?

One great piece of feedback on the MELT, written on a post-it note during a workshop introducing the models, was 'obvious'. That terse slight in many ways reflected that which the MELT was intended to convey: what educators do when they facilitate learning effectively. It is common that an educator looks at a version of MELT and says 'this is what I'm already doing!' That is perfect, for MELT provides an articulation of what educators often do implicitly and makes it explicit. For the person who said 'obvious', the question is whether their teaching approach is as obvious to their students or colleagues as it is to them. The answer is probably 'no'.

Educators use MELT for guidance when they perceive a need to move from leaving understanding implicit to making it explicit, in order to

(1) improve their awareness of their own practice and its connection to theory;
(2) enhance student metacognition, especially students' regulation of their own learning;
(3) connect disparate teaching energies, practices, sectors and theories.

As noted in earlier chapters, *learning autonomy* in MELT is not a characteristic that increases linearly, but a relationship: between students, between students and teachers, and between students and concepts. Engaged teachers attend implicitly to *learning autonomy*, because it is fundamental to ownership of the learning enterprise. MELT supports an explicit exploration of *learning autonomy*.

7.1 Autonomy: Engaged Learning, Engaged Teaching

A lot was made in the previous chapters about the *continuum of learning autonomy*. Chapter 2 discussed the continuum in relation to students and Chaps. 4 and 5 discussed it in relation to theory and action research. To reiterate here, autonomy in MELT is not an attribute to be attained to or an optimum level of guidance. A continuum suggests that there is a broad spectrum of possibilities, where all parts of the continuum are vital for learning: there is nothing inherently superior about *initiate* on

© The Author(s) 2020   131
J. Willison, *The Models of Engaged Learning and Teaching*,
SpringerBriefs in Education, https://doi.org/10.1007/978-981-15-2683-1_7

this continuum, nor is there anything implicitly lesser about emulate. The important thing is to ask frequently, 'how much guidance do these students need?' Autonomy in MELT depends on the relationship between learners and what is learned, where it is learned and who it is learned with. Learning autonomy distinctly ebbs and flows in a tidal zone, moving from low autonomy to high autonomy and back.

Measuring or pinning down *learning autonomy* is awkward, because it is a messy and recursive concept... Yet autonomy is absolutely central to daily teaching and learning. Because *learning autonomy* is a 'relationship term' in MELT, not an absolute quality, students don't *become* autonomous. Rather, they operate at times with higher levels of autonomy, depending on their familiarity with context and the rigour needed in the situation, and they frequently cycle back to lower levels of autonomy in less familiar contexts. This is what we found with employed graduates, who shuttle back and forth between different levels of autonomy in employment, showing that autonomy is non-linear and context-specific [2]. If MELT helps educators understand how much *learning autonomy* is required by a student, that 'measurement' can make a lot of sense for those who know and understand the context and inform teaching practices in practical ways. However, to say 'x% of students were working with high levels of autonomy' does not communicate anything meaningful to those without knowledge of the context.

In practical ways, MELT promotes constructive alignment to engineer quality, engaged learning. For example, MELT can inspire cognitive and affective learning outcomes or goals (Chap. 1), inform the design of face-to-face, online and blended learning environments (Chap. 3), inform the assessment of learning (Chap. 3) and help structure evaluative elements of course effectiveness (Chap. 5). However, constructive alignment only comes to life through the efforts of engaged teachers, for it requires teacher care and empowerment to realistically engage learners.

The MELT are used in a variety of ways for teaching, learning and researching, and this necessarily includes the assessment of student learning. Crucially, the *continuum of learning autonomy* suggests a student move from reliance on the teacher for feedback towards self-assessment, and back again in fresh contexts. Assessment rubrics, each informed by the six facets of MELT but with performance criteria made specific to a task, provide something in common between assignments. Such rubrics also provide something specific to that task alone. MELT rubrics straddle the middle ground between rubrics that are too specific to allow students to generalise their learning from it [3] and those that are too general and therefore provide little guidance. Importantly, when students use teacher feedback from one assignment to improve a subsequent assignment, the connections between assignments due to MELT make a substantial difference [4]. As students calibrate to teacher expectations using MELT-informed rubrics, they become more realistic in their self-assessment according to the rubric, and more able to give useful feedback to peers [5]. As shown in Chap. 3, an effective technique is to allocate marks to students' *response* to peer feedback, as well as marks for the feedback they give to others, as opposed to students allocating marks to students.

While this book has emphasised *learning* autonomy, teachers themselves need to model different levels of autonomy. Autonomy and ownership is a crucial dimension for teachers, because the MELT only work when educators make the models their own. If we want students to become increasingly autonomous and take risks in learning, then teachers themselves must have a license to act autonomously, at times, in order to show students what autonomy looks like. There is a need, then, to consider factors that increase or decrease *teacher* autonomy, because this implicitly affects teacher engagement and effectiveness.

When teachers do not show initiative or willingness to improvise, this may speak to the nature of the systems they teach in. This nature is often determined by what learning institutions reward and what the consequences of non-compliance are. Curriculum developers and policymakers should consider factors that mediate for and against teacher autonomy and ownership, including curriculum and quality assurance processes created for course, program and institution level.

MELT's *facets* articulated along the *continuum of learning autonomy* provide a framing that is 'sufficiently well structured' and 'sufficiently nebulous', as an educator said [6]. Another educator likened MELT to a thin silver wire providing the structure in which shimmery soap bubbles can emerge [7]. As the MELT draws on 100 years of educational research and practice, it contains nothing of a surprise in its separate elements. Rather, it is the juxtaposition of the facets with the levels of *learning autonomy* that makes the MELT distinctive in structure. But it is the educators who care, and their students, who make the MELT fluid through human interactions.

Overall, the MELT help to:

1. Envisage connections by providing a conceptualisation that holds in tension disparate educational practitioners', administrators, communities and researchers' perspectives.
2. Join together separate disciplinary and transdisciplinary usage.
3. Map the educational landscape, because they are informed by numerous educational theories, conceptual frameworks and practices.
4. Spiral through education and become a thinking routine, from primary school to Ph.D. level.
5. Delineate *learning autonomy*, unpacking how much guidance learners and teachers need.
6. Differentiate the curriculum, where the consideration of autonomy promotes an understanding of how to manage the curriculum for gifted and talented students, students with learning disabilities, and the full range of 'average' students.
7. Couple cognitive and affective learning, foregrounding the relationship between these domains
8. Prompt ethical, social and culturally minded teaching and learning.
9. Pose seven probing questions to teachers and students that are key across all educational contexts.
10. Materialise in audience-dependent ways, where educators adapt and articulate their own MELT, fit to the context and audience, even as the nature of the six *facets* and of the *continuum of learning autonomy* are maintained.

11. Engage teachers by absolutely relying on their professional sense of identity and care as they use their own adaptations of MELT to engage learners in the development of sophisticated thinking.

The four contemporary issues this book addressed were the following:

- Enabling educators to help students think in sophisticated ways.
- Connecting different aspects of education so that they mutually reinforce and complement each other.
- Deepening educators' understanding of the dimensions of student autonomy in learning.
- Engaging with educational theory in ways that make practical sense to educators.

How much guidance do educators need to so enable, connect, deepen, and engage? The answer is in your hands.

7.2 Conclusion: Structure Provided, Creativity Needed

The characteristics of MELT are based on 100 years of education research and mirror 100,000 years of human learning as experienced by 100 billion *Homo sapiens*. The next billion brains born from 2023 to 2030 need something different to those which have already been born. Existing members of our species brought us to the amazing creativity, adaptability, and problem-solving that will enable, in all likelihood, a human population of 8 billion alive in 2023. However, despite the massive problem-solving endeavour of our species, we are facing the catastrophic consequences of our solutions.

We need some guidance towards a mode of learning that will help the next billion brains, at the very least, to do no further damage to our world. We need to earn the name *sapiens*. MELT provides this guidance in a conceptual manner, but this guidance should not be represented as a set of rules or mandates. The MELT's adaptable structure absolutely requires the breath of creativity to bring it to life in particular subjects, disciplines and contexts. The MELT are fully dependent on *Homo sapiens'* willingness to adapt, to heat solid structures with the warmth of human interaction until conversations become fluid, and then crystallise in new shapes for student learning. If there are any things that are unique about the MELT, these include the articulation of the *facets* of sophisticated thinking along the *continuum of learning autonomy*, and the consequent way the models are able to simply connect theories with theories and theories with practice. The MELT's shared questions are effective prompts to engage teaching and learning. They continuously ask teachers and students, 'What will we use? What do we trust? How do we arrange? What does it mean? How do we relate? How much guidance?' and especially, 'What is our purpose?'

Melting, flowing, shaping and crystallising need to happen time and again, so that each of the MELT suits its context and is renewed when there are changes in that context. Each adapted MELT model interlinks conceptually with all other MELTs, and can help teachers and students make the connection across education's years, subjects, ideologies, and contexts. The MELT provide the adaptive fluidity we need to conceptualise the coherent and connected learning journey needed for the billion brains born from 2023. The children of Kevin, Shelly and Tara could be beneficiaries of an adept use of MELT, enabling them to experience and perceive their own forest of engaged learning. If those billion brains experience a coherent and connected curriculum, they may become sophisticated thinkers who craft solutions that first cause no harm. As they become the generation to lead us globally, they could pull us back from inevitable, accelerating, planetary degradation so that we all may enjoy a more evitable Earth trajectory. Remaining endangered habitats may be preserved despite increased human population and polar ice might remain frozen, because education, early childhood to Ph.D. is fluidly connected with the MELT.

References

1. Einstein Bubble in Cartoon: Einstein, A. (2010). *The ultimate quotable Einstein*. Princeton, NJ: Princeton University Press.
2. Willison, J., Sabir, F., & Thomas, J. (2017). Shifting dimensions of autonomy in students' research and employment. *Higher Education Research & Development, 36*(2), 430–443.
3. Adcroft, A. (2011). The mythology of feedback. *Higher Education Research & Development, 30*(4), 405–419.
4. Willison, J. (2012). When academics integrate research skill development in the curriculum. *Higher Education Research and Development, 31*(6), 905–919.
5. Wu, C., Chanda, E., & Willison, J. (2014). Implementation and outcomes of online self and peer assessment on group based honours research projects. *Assessment & Evaluation in Higher Education, 39*(1), 21–37.
6. Willison, J., & Buisman Pijlman, F. (2016). Ph.D. prepared: Research skill development across the undergraduate years. *International Journal of Researcher Development, 7*(1), 63–83.
7. Wisker, G. (2018). Frameworks and freedoms: Supervising research learning and the undergraduate dissertation. *Journal of University Teaching and Learning Practice, 15*(4), 2.

Glossary of MELT Terms

Analyse: to break down into constituent parts and pull together again in ways that show relationships. In quantitative research, these relationships involve *trends*. In qualitative research, these relationships involve *themes*. There is a close and recursive relationship between *analyse* and *organise*. Moreover, at times, analysis has strong *evaluative* elements; however, at other times they are distinctly different.

Apply: in the context of a learning task, put current knowledge and understanding into use cognitively, affectively and/or physically. Also put newly-developed knowledge into use in the context of a future task or problem.

Autonomy: the extent to which students drive the sophisticated thinking processes in MELT, which is related to the extent to which educators set the learning environment parameters.

Cognitive Load Theory (John Sweller): Human Working Memory has a small capacity and easy to overload with incoming information, especially multi-sensory information.

Communicate: ongoing process from start to finish of own or team's articulations, written, spoken and portrayed, with active listening and response. Frequently this leads to products for an audience, who may provide part of a feedback loop for ongoing improvement.

Connectivism (George Sieman's): Information and knowledge are available to a learner from networks of people, devices and other sources, and often accessed at time of need.

Clarify: fine-tune one's purpose through a deepened understanding of sophisticated thinking.

Constructive: a desire to build up, not merely to persuade or gain self-benefit.

Creative: making something new to oneself and one's team, whether through the synthesis of parts or from scratch; not mimicry.

Curious: intoxicated by an issue or phenomenon and inspired to pursue it; not disengaged.

Determined: continuing until one has an appropriate resolution; not a gathering of information or generation of data that is slapdash.

J. Willison, *The Models of Engaged Learning and Teaching*,
SpringerBriefs in Education, https://doi.org/10.1007/978-981-15-2683-1

Discerning: insightful look at information and people, not gullibly consumed or tricked into participating.

Embark: to set off on a learning journey, frequently involving re-embarking.

Engagement: frequently socially interactive and always minds-on cognitively and affectively. Engagement in MELT involves social, cognitive and emotional values and attitudes about *learning* and about *teaching*. The details of the engagement are provided in MELT's six facets of learning and extent of autonomy.

Facet: one face of the precious jewel of sophisticated thinking.

Harmonising: taking clutter and wreaking order on it, taking discord and making beautiful connections.

Learning: going to a conceptual and affective place where one has not been before, requiring and enabling sophisticated thinking. Brain-wise, this is the result of the formation and consolidation of synapses in multiple locations in the brain.

Machine Learning: Discernment of trends and themes from data inputted and collected to synthesise understanding, with potential to influence subsequent decisions, actions and data gathering.

Machine Teaching: Machines programmed to teach and/or using Machine Learning to teach in ways that increasingly target 'optimised' learning for each student.

Manage: working with timeframes, teams and resources so that they serve and do not hinder that which is embarked on.

Organise: arrangements that bring time, resources, information and data into shape in a way that is conducive to making sense of information and data.

Reflective Practitioner: Donald Schon's practitioner, who, facing uncertainties reflects 'in-action' and later looks back to learn from the situation, reflecting 'on-action'. This self-teaching without external inputs is powerful and meaning-oriented.

Scope for autonomy: the extent of the structure and guidance which is *given* to students in any learning tasks. This does not guarantee anything about the extent of student autonomy *realised*.

Sophisticated thinking: the thinking required for problem solving, critical thinking, evidence based decision making, researching, understanding and metacognition, to name a few.

Synthesise: pull together disparate parts to make a whole that is new to oneself, one's team or one's audience. Typically a creative act.

Teaching: guiding others towards a conceptual and affective place they have never been before.

Threshold Concepts (Ernst Meyer and Ray Land): Core concepts in any subject or discipline, that enable or prevent students from deep learning.

Index

© The Author(s), under exclusive license to Springer Nature Singapore Pte Ltd. 2020
J. Willison, *The Models of Engaged Learning and Teaching*,
SpringerBriefs in Education, https://doi.org/10.1007/978-981-15-2683-1